First Communion *and Beyond*

A Family's Guide to Eucharistic Joy

Tommy *and* Katie McGrady
Hosts of Family Mass Prep on Hallow

Nihil Obstat: Reverend Monsignor Michael Heintz, PhD
Censor Librorum

Imprimatur: Most Reverend Kevin C. Rhoades
Bishop of Fort Wayne–South Bend
Given at Fort Wayne, Indiana, on September 18, 2025

Founded in 1865, Ave Maria Press is a ministry of the United States Province of Holy Cross.

www.avemariapress.com

Paperback: ISBN-13 978-1-64680-437-5

E-book: ISBN-13 978-1-64680-438-2

Cover image © Getty Images.

Cover design by Brianna Dombo and Christopher D. Tobin.

Text design by Christopher D. Tobin.

Printed and bound in the United States of America.

Library of Congress Cataloging-in-Publication Data is available.

"As the mom of a seven-year-old who will be making his First Communion this spring, I am so grateful to have the help of Tommy and Katie McGrady and their wonderful book *First Communion and Beyond: A Family's Guide to Eucharistic Joy*. It's faithful, practical, and, most of all, written from the perspective of parents who are in the trenches with us, striving to raise joyful, healthy children who love Jesus and the Catholic faith. In short, it's a treasure!"

Emily Stimpson Chapman
Catholic author, speaker, and cohost of the *Visitation Sessions* podcast

"As Catholic parents, we want to do everything we can to help prepare our kids to receive Jesus at their First Communion, but the question is how. In *First Communion and Beyond*, Tommy and Katie McGrady take out the guesswork with a beautiful and feasible at-home guide that any parent can follow."

Lisa and Kevin Cotter
Host of the Hallow app series *Hallowed Be Thy Day*; head of studios at Hallow

"It is no small thing to welcome voices of guidance and accompaniment into the sacred space of family life and the formation of children concerning the source and summit of our faith—the Eucharist. I am confident that Tommy and Katie McGrady are worthy guides for you during this sacred time. In *First Communion and Beyond*, they mine the treasures of ordinary moments in their own family life and offer you practical guidance—including sample scripts for various moments! They help you learn to hold space for and encourage children's wonder and their questions about Jesus in the Eucharist. Their daughter Rose is a profound witness in her courage to ask questions about the mysteries of our faith. Her younger sister, Clare, is a profound witness in her trust of the mysteries of the faith. May the witness of the McGrady family be an encouragement to you as you allow this time in your family life to be a renewal of wonder, curiosity, joy, confidence, and faith before Jesus in the Eucharist."

Sr. Josephine Garrett, CSFN
Licensed mental health counselor, host of the *Hope Stories* podcast,
and author of *Wilderness Within*

"Talking to our kids about the source and summit of our faith can be incredibly intimidating, and it can also function as a bit of a mirror, exposing what we believe about something we don't necessarily talk about a lot on a daily basis. Now the McGradys have created something that not only will help children learn how to enter the Mass from their young perspectives—it will also help parents rediscover a childlike faith in the greatest miracle we all bear witness to every week: the Eucharist."

Matt Maher

Catholic recording artist and songwriter

"Catholic families today need this book! With practical tools and heartfelt guidance, it equips parents to walk with their children not only on the day of First Communion but also throughout the lifelong journey of faith that follows. Blending down-to-earth reflections with humorous and poignant stories, this book nurtures the faith of young children, their parents, and families who together ensure no one is left behind! Thank you, McGradys! What a treasure this book will be!"

Elisabeth Williams

Cofounder and director of mission integration at Catholic Concepts

"This book had me laughing but also in tears several times—what a treasure it will be for families walking with a child toward First Communion! Tommy and Katie McGrady share personal stories that are both relatable and seamlessly connected to scripture and Church teaching. Parents who often feel ill-equipped will find themselves encouraged and formed in faith alongside their children, discovering that they, too, are invited, welcomed, and nourished at the Lord's table."

Christie McGee

Director of children and family ministry at
St. Joseph Catholic Church in Richardson, Texas

"The Church sets before us some exalted mysteries: God is three and one; the Lord took human flesh; the bread and wine become his Body and Blood. While these mysteries lie well beyond our comprehension, God still prompts us to grasp something of their beauty. In this book, Tommy and Katie McGrady lay out the essentials of Eucharistic worship with stories and images that will cause both parents and first communicants to marvel. For as exalted as the mysteries are, they are still somehow ours for the taking."

Fr. Gregory Pine, OP

Instructor of dogmatic and moral theology at the Dominican House of Studies
and assistant director of the Thomistic Institute

To Sister Lilianna Petra, our Wawa,
whose devotion to the Eucharist
has helped us all grow more in love with the Lord.
Thanks for showing us how to love Jesus,
who tends gardens and builds temples,
with our whole hearts.

Contents

Prologue

Jesus at 3939 Lake Street, Lake Charles, Louisiana

Katie: Jesus Outside

Our morning commute to school takes Rose, Clare, and me right past Our Lady Queen of Heaven (OLQH) Catholic Church. This was my childhood parish, the place where I grew up, worked as a youth minister, married Tommy, and where our girls were baptized. Adorning the outside of the church, right above the Lake Street entrance, is a giant crucifix, facing toward the busy street. Every morning as we drive past OLQH, we wave and say, "Hi, Jesus." On the mornings I forget to wave to Jesus, I'm quickly reprimanded with a swift kick to my seat by the scrupulous and attentive five-year-old sitting in the booster seat just behind me.

These little "Hi, Jesus" moments began somewhat in jest. One normal morning, our daughter Rose—only four years old at the time—noticed Jesus there on the cross, and she casually remarked, "Jesus looks so sad today," sparking a long conversation about whether Jesus is sad every day since he's hanging on that cross on the outside wall. In her mind, that meant Jesus never got to go inside, and that probably made him sad. We had a glum drop-off that particular morning and Rose just couldn't comprehend why Jesus had to stay outside, even if it happened to be raining.

The following morning, when it was in fact raining, I was prepared for tears as we drove past the church, waiting for Rose to notice Jesus on that outside cross, soaking wet. But as we drove by, Rose simply looked out the minivan window, saw him up there on the cross in the rain, and waved and said, “Hi, Jesus,” as if it was the most normal thing in the world. The next morning, bright and sunny with not a cloud in the sky, she did it again. “Hi, Jesus.” And so began our morning ritual of driving past the church and greeting Our Lord and Savior with a wave and a “Hi, Jesus,” our morning made better with a moment of communion in the Lord.

I didn’t think much of it at the time, though I’d love to claim now that it was this profound Catholic parenting win. But truthfully, it was just something simple and sweet happening in our minivan on the way to school. Each school day we waved “hi” to the crucifix—first named “sad Jesus”—hanging on the outside of a church that meant, and still means, so much to our family. Then, a few weeks later, at a Saturday evening Mass in that same church with my mom and dad on one end of the pew, Tommy, the girls, and I beside them, Rose and I both experienced a new depth of realization about the presence of Jesus in our midst.

At the moment of the consecration, as our pastor, Msgr. Torres, elevated the host after saying the words “This is my Body . . .,” I leaned forward and whispered into the ear of my then one-year-old, Clare, who was snuggled against me, “Look, Bear, that’s Jesus.” She looked up to the front of the Church, suddenly more fascinated by what was happening in the sanctuary than with the patterns of the wood grain on the pew she’d been attempting to scratch with her fingernails. “Dat’s Jesus?” she asked. “That’s Jesus, yes. Can you wave hi to Jesus?”

I waited for Clare to lift her chubby little hand to wave, but instead, I felt a hard tug on my sweater, glanced down, and saw Rose looking up at me, stunned. “Mom, *that’s Jesus*?” she whispered, trying her hardest not to speak at full volume, and woefully failing.

More than a few chuckles broke out around us, and I quickly whispered back, “Yes, bud, that’s Jesus.” Then I was thinking about how to more fully explain this complex, yet foundational, Catholic belief that what looks and tastes like and seems to be merely a flat, round wafer is indeed Christ Jesus made present to us in the Eucharistic mystery. But before I could say anything else, Rose turned back toward the altar, her little face practically glowing with pride as she gazed at the chalice being held high for all to see, and she smiled. It was the biggest smile I’d ever seen on her little face, every tooth showing as her grin spread wide.

Something was happening in my daughter's young mind, the gears clearly turning as she looked toward the sanctuary. Maybe I wouldn't have to explain it after all. The religious sensibilities of children are far more profound and rich than we adults often comprehend, so maybe she just had some inborn understanding of the Eucharist, of Christ's presence in Holy Communion. St. Carlo Acutis did. St. Thérèse of Lisieux did. Why not my Rose? A mom can hope.

As soon as the cantor began to sing, "Save us, Savior of the world," Rose looked at me, still beaming, and said very confidently—and very loudly—"Mom, Jesus got to come inside! He isn't stuck outside on the wall anymore!" And as soon as Monsignor elevated the consecrated bread and wine (the Blessed Sacrament) and invited us to "Behold the Lamb of God, who takes away the sins of the world," both my daughters waved and whisper-shouted, "Hi, Jesus!"

Turns Out, Jesus Has an Address

While it is precious to see a tiny child wave at the tabernacle or at a crucifix hanging high above a church entrance, or blow a kiss at an image of Jesus pointing to his own Sacred Heart, there is also something quite profound unfolding when a little one reminds us big ones of a stark yet comforting truth: Jesus is real, Jesus is present, and Jesus dwells *somewhere*. Yes, Christ is in our hearts and alive in our minds, and all of creation shouts the grandeur of the Lord. But also, Jesus is present at 3939 Lake Street in Lake Charles, Louisiana, in a silver tabernacle with a relief of the Last Supper on the front doors. And Jesus is present in every church and in every tabernacle all around the world, where bread is taken up by the priest, consecrated by the power of the Holy Spirit, broken, and shared. At Mass we receive and consume Christ, Our Lord, present in Holy Communion. And Jesus Christ, Our Lord, is present in tabernacles in parish churches and grand cathedrals alike all around the world—there for us to adore in devotion outside of Mass.

Jesus *is* somewhere, and we can go *there*. We can say hi even if we're just waving to the crucifix high up on an outside wall. Jesus is real and present to us in the physical elements of the Eucharist. Of all the things we are called to teach our children about our Catholic faith, the mystery and gift of the Eucharist certainly tops the list. But this can never be thought of as a one-and-done effort. Rather, that we encounter the living Christ in the Eucharist is a belief requiring a lifetime of pondering and of saying "Amen" to that mystery in tiny steps all along the way. As parents, we help our children learn about the Eucharist, and we help them learn the appropriate reverence needed to joyfully meet and receive Christ in Holy Communion.

When we ask the Church to baptize our children, we accept the responsibility and receive the gift to be teachers to our children. We teach them about Christ present not only at Mass, but while we're at the dinner table, watching a movie, cuddled up on the couch with them, on the playground, or out for a family walk with the lollygagging four-year-old insisting she can keep up on her bike, then abandoning it to Dad's trusty carrying skills.

And we have the joy of helping our children learn to see Jesus present in friends and strangers and clerks at the grocery store. Probing the mystery of the Eucharist is a lifelong adventure, and we parents get to journey alongside our little ones as they begin their own explorations. What a grace! What a blessing!

Even after Rose realized Jesus was actually *inside* the Church, and not just stuck on a cross outside, she continued to wave "hi" to Jesus (and still does to this day) as we drove past the church on our way to school each morning. And that brief little hello to the Lord, first thing in the morning, has been an anchor for all of us in the minivan. It keeps Jesus present and centered in our hearts throughout the day. It reminds us that Jesus is *always* with us—as we go to all the places we have to go and do all the things we do each day. When we realize and understand that this is what the Lord wants for each of us more than anything else—to be close to him and receive him into every part of our being—then everything changes. No longer is Jesus a sad figure on the outside of a building, nor some distant part of a Bible story. Rather, he is real, present, receivable, and waiting for you and for me.

It is no small task to articulate that meaningfully, and helpfully, to a child who, in our case, first thought Jesus was stuck on the outside of a building. We have to bring Jesus down from that cross on the outside wall and out of the pretty pictures. In some ways this is the entire project of First Communion preparation: helping our children take Jesus from the abstractions of what we believe about him and instead see him fully present in the everyday realities of their young lives. Preparing for First Communion ought to teach our children—and remind us—how to know and love Jesus in their hearts, in the scriptures, in the Eucharist, and in all the other people life brings their way.

We had the chance to do this with our daughter Rose, as we helped her grow to understand the gift of the Eucharist. Along the way, we also developed a deeper love and devotion to the Eucharist and learned a good deal about what we Catholics believe as well. Our spiritual journey as a family during Rose's preparation for First Communion brought us one of the most intense, joyful, challenging, and life-giving projects of our parenthood thus far. This little book is the story of how we helped our daughter prepare for First Communion, and how we parents began to approach the Eucharist with a new understanding, wonder, and enthusiasm in our own hearts. It's the book we hoped to be able to read as we were walking this road of First Communion prep. Since we couldn't find that book, we decided to write it. We hope it helps you and your family as well.

Using This Book

Each chapter of this book is focused on one aspect of what we believe about the Eucharist. By reading and reflecting on stories from our family life, as well as learning about what Catholics believe from some of our favorite Bible passages, we are convinced that you will grow in your faith along with your child.

Each chapter unfolds in five parts, each of which is a tool for your family's spiritual growth. We hope and pray these tools will help you better navigate the way to your child's First Communion and renew your spiritual life at the same time. We will be walking with you in spirit as you grow in your own personal faith and devotion to the Eucharist as adults and specifically as parents, godparents, grandparents, or other adult travelers with those getting reading for First Communion. We want to help you more fully participate in the Mass, while also helping your child prepare to receive Jesus in the Eucharist for the first time.

Five Tools for Your Family's Spiritual Growth

1. **Joining Our Stories to the Church's Story:** We'll tell you a story from our family and link it to the Catholic spiritual and sacramental Tradition—the stories of our Church. We hope these get you reflecting on your family life.

2. **Learning from Scripture:** Here we'll take you through parts of the Bible that we find helpful in trying to more fully understand and love the Eucharist. There is some parent-friendly commentary about connections between our homes and the Bible stories we'll explore.
3. **Thinking and Growing as Parents:** Here we give you some prompts for reflecting on and talking about your faith.
4. **Growing Together as Parents and Children:** In this part, we provide guidance and a sample script for reflecting and talking with little ones about the scripture passage for the chapter and how it can help us better understand the Eucharist.
5. **Praying as a Family:** Here we invite you to close the conversation between parents and child with a simple prayer from us, or to pray in your own way.

From Our Family to Yours

The Eucharist was a priority for us long before we walked the road to a First Communion as parents. But now the Eucharist has become a priority within our home, even more than we'd imagined it could or would be. This time of preparation gave us a renewed sense of purpose and joy as a Catholic family—a domestic church. Even after years in education, youth ministry, and working with various other apostolates in the Church, we realized we had a lot of room to grow ourselves. It was not until we had to talk about the immense wonder and mystery of the Eucharist on a second-grade level that its majesty and meaning began to click in deeper ways for us. It's hard to say who grew more, Rose or us. Walking a faith journey with a child to First Communion and then beyond it is an immeasurable privilege, one that we hope and pray will help you grow more deeply in your own devotion and faith. Have an amazing, grace-filled experience worthy of the children of God!

1.

Come as You Are

Joining Our Stories to the Church's Story

Katie: "That's Warm. And Wet!"

I'd set their clothes out the night before, determined that we wouldn't be late the next morning. Preplanned outfits would mitigate any disasters, for both children and parents, and so hanging on the closet door were matching dresses for our girls with outfits in complementary colors for Tommy and me in our room, also ready to go. I was nothing if not prepared, and family photos on a Sunday morning would go smoothly if I had any control of the situation.

We'd take family photos a couple of times a year, the same photographer making the girls giggle and twirl around session after session. This year, for her springtime picture sessions, she was offering a package for families to take photos at a gorgeous park with a 150-year-old oak tree, complete with the chance for the kids to hold bunny rabbits. Idyllic!

And so, with the plans in place, the photos scheduled for 8:45 in the morning, I knew we'd be finished by 9:15 at the latest, and then we'd head off to the cathedral right around the corner for 9:30 a.m. Mass. Luckily the priest also happened to be our youngest daughter's godfather. Family photos to start, Mass with Fr. Godfather to finish, perhaps we'd even splurge and get some Sunday smoothies on the way home after. I love it when a plan comes together.

Much to my surprise, our morning of getting ready and out the door was relatively smooth. Setting out the outfits and finding shoes the night before had helped tremendously, and other than one slight battle about preferred hairstyles from the six-year-old, we left our house at 8:20 with plenty of time to get to the photo spot.

"Mom, are the bunnies going to bite me?" Rose, ever concerned about safety, had been asking questions all morning about proper handling and care of bunnies used in seasonal family photos.

"No, bud, not if you're gentle with them," I assured her for the tenth time.

"Will dey wike me!?" Clare piped up. "Because I wike dem!" My nature- and animal-loving child, looking resplendent in her denim jacket and clear jelly sandals, was less concerned about safety and more interested in whether the bunnies would become her lifelong pals. I was fairly convinced she'd try to keep one of the bunnies, so we'd gently reminded her, repeatedly, that the bunnies would be staying with Ms. Kennedy and not coming home with us. She was certain we weren't serious.

We arrived early, waited patiently as the family before us wrapped up their session, and as soon as the photographer gave us the go-ahead, the girls raced off to the little holding pen where three bunnies—one gray, one brown, and one speckled with black and white patches—huddled together. They were precious, these little Easter creatures sitting in the grass, munching on some greens, far more adorable than any Bugs Bunny episode would have you think bunny rabbits could be. Rose softly pet their heads, cooing to them not to be scared. Clare tried to climb into the pen, convinced she could become one with the rabbits. Tommy and I just stood there and laughed, hopeful that whatever photos Ms. Kennedy might capture would be a good snapshot of the girls at this age.

"Okay, McGradys, over here!" she shouted to us.

We made our way over to the oak tree, lined up holding hands, and started walking toward our photographer as she snapped away, the sounds of the shutter floating through the muggy air, our smiles hopefully hiding the sweat beginning to pool on our faces and arms. Louisiana in April can either be perfectly temperate or so humid it feels like you're walking into a damp washcloth. Today was a wet-washcloth day. But the reward was coming. Bunny rabbits. If we could endure this heat, for even just a few more moments, each of the girls would get to sit in a child-size rocking chair and hold a bunny, an idyllic spring, Southern moment captured forever in a photo I'd surely frame (or at least make the lock screen of my phone for a while).

Finally finished with the family shots, Ms. Kennedy instructed Rose to go pick which bunny she wanted to hold, which led to Clare's immediate insistence that she would be holding all three bunnies, one at a time, and then all together. Holding her bunny with both hands, snuggling it close to her face, Rose declared, "Look, Mom, he's calm!" It was a perfect spring scene, as if Rose was a born bunny farmer. A few moments later, Clare shouted, "They weally weally wike me!" as she sat in the pen, each bunny hopping over to her and slowly climbing into her lap. She was happy as can be, bunnies all around her, a giant smile on her face. There they played, our two girls, in a bunny pen, on a perfectly muggy spring morning, twenty minutes before Sunday Mass was set to begin right down the street. *I hope I don't forget this*, I thought to myself as I watched the sweet moment.

"I think we got it!" Ms. Kennedy told us a few moments later, the kids and bunnies giggling as the camera shutter slowed.

"Can I hold one?" Tommy asked. "You don't have to take a picture or anything," he assured her as he reached down into the pen to pick up the speckled bunny. "They're just really cute," he murmured.

And then, in what can only be described as a perfect conflagration of chaos, as Tommy bent down to pick up the speckled bunny, Rose bent down to pick up the gray bunny. They bumped heads—hard—and Rose yelped at the top of her lungs. The bunny closest to her, clearly startled by the shout, bit her finger. She screamed again. Then, as Tommy was grasping onto the speckled bunny, who wiggled and thrashed out of his hands and back into Clare's little lap, he suddenly groaned, "Welp, that's warm. And wet!" He pulled his hand out of the pen and turned to Rose to check on her finger.

Clare, still sitting with the startled bunnies on her lap, began to cry, and as I reached into the pen to try to pick her up, she whimpered, "It's wet!" The speckled bunny hopped off, suddenly perfectly calm, while I pushed the brown and gray bunnies off of her. Either they were in shock or the most Zen bunnies I'd ever met, as neither seemed all that phased by the chaos of a screaming, freshly bitten child. As Clare stood up, I noticed a giant wet spot on the front of her dress. When she looked down, her tears began to fall as she whispered, "I sowwy, mom."

I held back laughter, biting my tongue to keep from chuckling as it dawned on me that the scenarios both my children had imagined came true: Rose had been bit by a bunny, and the bunnies had liked Clare so much that they'd peed all over her.

Traffic Cone-Orange

In thirty seconds, our perfectly put-together outfits had become unkempt, one of them wet with fresh bunny pee. Tommy consoled a weeping Rose, who was slowly convincing herself she now had a communicable disease from a bunny. He, too, was fighting laughter at the entire chaotic scene. Clare, soaked in the urine of the fluffy creatures with which she was obsessed, was still whimpering, clearly uncomfortable as the sour smell wafted up to her face.

I kicked into mom mode, realizing that she needed to be changed out of her outfit, Rose needed a bandage to feel somewhat better, Tommy and I both needed a private moment to laugh about the hilarity of the moment, and the photographer needed to be reassured we would not in any way sue her for the killer bunny bite.

We rushed back to the minivan, pulled out the emergency first aid kit, and tended to Rose's finger, and I began searching for the spare clothes that we usually kept in the van. The key word here is *usually*. I am, without fail, a diligent type A mom who, at any given moment, keeps a change of clothes for each of us in the minivan. There have been too many spill mishaps, potty accidents, and weather incidents not to warrant a spare shirt or pair of shorts in the van storage. So I opened the trunk box expecting to find the packing cube for the girls to be sitting right where I knew I'd left it. And when it wasn't where I'd left it, I suddenly remembered that I had removed it—the week before, in fact, when I had deep cleaned the van and made a mental note to change out the spare clothes to the right sizes for the girls who had, of course, grown. Standing there stunned and mad at myself for not remembering to replace the clothes, I looked down at Clare, covered in bunny urine, as she industriously stripped herself down to her Pull-Up, looking a little pitiful and impoverished.

Then she proudly announced, "I naked, Momma." No shame, that one.

"Who's naked?" I heard Tommy shout from the side, where he was still consoling the very upset Rose, who was now convinced all woodland creatures would hate her forever because she'd frightened the bunnies.

"No one. Well, Clare. I don't have spare clothes!" I shouted back.

"You always have spare clothes," he retorted, thinking I was joking.

"Not this time," I murmured, rummaging through the trunk box, hoping I would find *something*. And I did!

I found one single T-shirt, bright orange, an XL given to me by a youth group I'd met at a conference the summer before. I'd tossed it in the minivan when they'd given it to me and had completely forgotten about it. "HE IS OUR REFUGE" was printed across the front. On the back was a drawing of a monstrance (the sacred vessel used to hold the Blessed Sacrament for certain Eucharistic devotions), with "COME AS YOU ARE" in scripted font arched around the top of the image. "Welp," I muttered, grabbing the shirt, pulling it over our size 5T, three-year-old Clare, and bringing her over to the car seat to buckle her in.

For a brief moment, I'd convinced myself we should just call an audible, skip Mass altogether, apologize to Jesus for bunny-urine-family-photo mishaps, and end the whole shebang. But there was that shirt, with a reminder that the Lord, where he is, is my refuge and strength, and I, where I am, must go to him, just as I am. Or, in this case, I should bring my bunny-peed-upon child, just as she was. Even if it meant she had to wear a traffic-cone-colored T-shirt.

"Figure it out, babe?" Tommy asked as I buckled in.

"She's coming as she is, and it's just going to have to be fine," I said back, mad at myself for the mistake of cleaning out the spare clothes, but also slightly amused at the outcome. "Not how I thought our idyllic family photos before Mass would go."

Tommy glanced to the back seat—Rose with her injured finger, Clare with the bright-orange Jesus T-shirt—and finally let out the laugh he'd been holding back. I started to chuckle, too, and as we walked into the cathedral a few moments later—with three of us looking hot and sweaty and a bit unkempt in coordinated outfits and one of us in a traffic-cone-colored shirt with the Eucharist pictured on the back—I thought to myself, for the second time that morning, *I hope I don't forget this.*

Come As You Are

We show up to Mass, hopefully more or less on time, and slip into a pew, maybe kneel down to say a few prayers, and then sit there, waiting for things to begin. We bring our whole selves into that pew.

All the chaos of the previous events of the day, including biting, peeing bunny mishaps. We bring our anxieties and our worries and our fears. We're sitting there, to-do lists running through our minds, the projects of the week bouncing around our heads, the concerns we carry weighing on our hearts. We bring it all, and we come as we are. No one, least of all the Lord, expects us to just forget all of that the moment Mass begins.

In fact, we carry all of that with us, and Mass becomes the place where we can set it all down at the altar and offer it to the Lord. Mass is where we can encounter our living God and say, "Here I am. Here is all of me, messy and bunny bitten, with a bright orange T-shirt and unkempt hair." Mass is precisely the place to bring everything we don't want to (or even can't) forget and hand it over to Jesus. Then, as Mass begins, we make the Sign of the Cross, recalling that we belong to the Cross and to the Blessed Trinity in whose threefold name we gather to worship: Father, Son, and Holy Spirit. Next, we are greeted by the priest who reminds us that the Lord is with us. We respond in kind, praying that the Lord fills the priest's spirit. These words ought to comfort us even in the messiest of our messes. This greeting comes as a prayerful exchange, and when it is welcomed in, when it is received by us in gratitude, it can quiet the noise and bring peace into the chaos of all the stuff that may have followed us into church.

The Lord, our God—who has created us, loves us, draws us close, and desires to fill our hearts with joy—is with us. In that place, in that moment, the Lord is present, drawing us in, happy we are there. No matter what we're wearing, or how we got there, or what was happening before, or even what's to come later. In that moment, right then and there, the Lord is with us. We've come as we are, we've not forgotten everything that's followed us and that we're holding on to, and we meet the Lord who is waiting for us right there.

Mass doesn't begin with a command, or instructions, or exhortations. Mass begins with a reminder, a prayerful invitation, a greeting of love and fellowship. We then respond with a remarkable expression of our own desire for the well-being of the priest, who will lead us in our celebration of the Eucharistic liturgy. We pray that the Lord be with his spirit. In this mutual expression of the desire that the Lord be among us, in the very place where we behold him, adore him, worship, and receive him, we find that the Lord is already with us, just as we are. The question for us, then, is simple: *Do we want to be with him?*

Learning from Scripture

Behold the Lamb of God

There's one figure in scripture who, no matter which way you try to square the circle, is an odd duck. With a wardrobe of hair shirts and a diet of locusts and honey, the holy hipster of the gospels—John the Baptist—who leapt in his mother's womb upon encountering Jesus for the first time, serves as both an inspiration and a challenge to us. John gave his all to Jesus—his mission, his time, even his very life. He drew a following, but not for himself, never for himself, but always to be the voice crying out in the desert to prepare a way for the Lord—the one he knew intimately, loved deeply, and wanted others to know too. The Lord was with John the Baptist, and all he wanted was for others also to know the gift of that closeness, to know that the Lord was with them.

One day, as John was out baptizing and preaching with two of his disciples, he saw Jesus walk by, and he said, "Behold the Lamb of God" (John 1:36). Struck by the title given to this random passerby, the two disciples, Andrew and John, turn to see Jesus for the first time. Hearing John refer to Jesus as "the Lamb of God" would have made them wonder just what John meant. They likely wondered how this stranger might save them and their people.

Becoming curious, Andrew and John follow Jesus, and when he notices them, Jesus turns and asks, "What are you looking for?" An innocent enough question, it seems. But what a moment! Imagine being told, "There's the Lamb of God," and understanding that to mean, *one who will be sacrificed to save us*, then having that very man turn to you and ask what you're looking for! Was he wanting to help? Was he annoyed?

Having shown up by Jesus's side, clearly unprepared for any sort of in-depth conversation, perhaps even carrying all the noise and chaos and busyness of their full day into the interaction, Andrew and John blurt out, "Rabbi, where are you staying?" What a funny question! These men don't really know much about Jesus other than John the Baptist having called him the Lamb of God. And all they come up with is "Where are you staying"!

Did Jesus chuckle? Did he roll his eyes? Was he amused at their question, or perhaps perturbed? Was he used to odd questions from random men? Or, as is likely the case, did he know precisely what was in the heads and hearts of young John and eager Andrew? Here they stood, curious, waiting for an answer to a question they may not have thought much about, but that they asked anyway. They wanted to know where he was going, and that genuine curiosity sparks an answer that changes all of human history. "Come, and you will see," Jesus says to the two of them. A loaded answer for a seemingly simple question.

Jesus isn't going to give them an address. He isn't going to share his travel plans. This isn't a moment to share an itinerary, much less be planning one. Instead, Jesus, the Lamb of God they've just met—a teacher they've encountered because of a voice crying out in the wilderness—invites them to come with him. He can't really tell them *where*, but he will show them the way, and he will invite them to come along on the journey and into his ministry and mission.

"Come, and you will see," is a profound challenge to set everything aside and just go where the Lord invites us. Andrew and John, in that moment, are invited to bring their whole selves—all their mess, all their questions, all their own plans, to-do lists, hopes and fears and concerns—with them. Jesus doesn't say, "Go pack a bag, make some arrangements, and come back in a day or two." He doesn't tell them to go handle their affairs or finish up their projects. He doesn't ask them to clean up, or clear their minds. "Come, and you will see." Right now. Right away. At this moment. Come with me, in this place.

Four O'Clock in the Afternoon

This was almost certainly not the answer Andrew and John expected. You ask someone where they're staying expecting the name of an inn or the address of someone's home. But instead, these men receive a life-changing invitation from Jesus, to just go with him and see. Then Andrew and John just go. They go with Jesus, responding to his beautiful invitation with a willing and hopeful yes. They go, seemingly without hesitation or worry or fear.

It is interesting to note that the Gospel of John records the time of this interaction between Jesus, Andrew, and John: "It was about four in the afternoon" (John 1:39). Many scholars believe this is a clue that sundown was near, which meant the Sabbath was soon to begin, bringing rest. What better way to take such rest than with this man who might be the long-awaited Messiah?

The Gospel records the time of day much like we mark down or remember the time of a child's birth or where we were when we met the love of our life. John remembers the sun was starting to set in the sky, that the long day was concluding, and he documents the time. Andrew, so moved by this encounter and being invited to go and see with Jesus, rushes back to his brother, Simon, and tells him, "We have found the Messiah." He knows that Jesus is someone to note, someone to follow, someone his brother needs to know too.

Every time we go to Mass, celebrating and receiving the Eucharist, we hear the same thing spoken to us: "Come, and see." We are gathered together, invited to go with the Lord, to meet him, to encounter and be with him, to receive him. At the very beginning of Mass, we are welcomed just as we are, our whole selves—messes and all. When we hear the priest's greeting, we can trust, as Andrew and John did, that the Lord Jesus is truly with us. He is within each of us as individual members of his Body, the Church, and he is there among us, binding us together in love. As each Mass begins, we can rest and rejoice in knowing that "Jesus is here, I am here, we are here, and we will follow him to see what he has to offer us."

Come and You Will See

Far more often than either of us like to admit, the opening minutes of Mass are a bit frantic for our family. We're all getting situated in the pew, there's usually a request for a bathroom break, and it's not uncommon for a child's shoe to fall off after she begs to be held. Then, from the priest up in the sanctuary, we are warmly and firmly reminded that God is with us just as we are, right there, right then.

But no matter how chaotic getting out of the house may have been, or how tired we may be, or even how prepared (or unprepared) we feel to be sitting in Mass at that moment, we are there. We've accepted once again the invitation to come and see what life is like with Jesus. So, there we find ourselves. We go to see where Jesus goes and how we can follow. Sometimes, we go and see at four o'clock in the afternoon like Andrew and John in our Bible story. Usually, we go at nine o'clock on Sunday mornings, no matter what has happened beforehand.

Just being in church for Mass on a late Saturday afternoon or a Sunday morning is commendable in a culture where it is so easy to fill our family calendars with sporting events and practices, social outings, yard work, housework, overdue shopping, or even long-needed downtime. It is no small thing to have chosen to be at Sunday Mass. So, when the priest greets you in the name of the whole Church, try to settle into the moment, knowing Jesus is there, being Lord. And you are there, being you and responding to the priest's greeting with your own prayerful greeting. And the Lord is with us all, and we are with him, and now we can begin to praise and petition, listen and learn, honor, receive, and share the Lord, who invites us to come—just as we are—and see who he is and what he has to offer us.

You Made It!

This is an important reality to hold in our hearts, as hard as it may be. We don't have to show up to Mass looking perfect, or even feeling perfect. It is important to take time to quiet our hearts and try to settle ourselves into prayer and worship when we arrive, and it's certainly worth noting that there are a few things we can do to make that easier long before we walk into our churches.

Before Mass, we try to go screen-free as a family, for the morning, or at least an hour before we leave. We give up our phones, trying to avoid texting and social media, we keep the television turned off, and we try to embrace some quiet, in every aspect of our lives. This is a time to just settle, even just our physical bodies, before we go to see the Lord. We do our level best to listen to either praise and worship or *Family Mass Prep* on the Hallow app on the drive to our parish church. We try to remember—and hope that you can, too—that the first and most important thing when you arrive at Mass, and as Mass begins, is that you are there, and praise God for that. You showed up. You responded to the Lord's invitation. You made it!

As parents, we get to set the tone for our families when we go to Mass. We can, even if there are moments of chaos and craziness on the trip there, enter into Mass with joy, excitement, hopefulness, and peace. Even if the arriving moments were a bit chaotic, and even if there were a few tears shed along the way because one child didn't want to wear a certain pair of shoes—all those moments of family craziness, occasional whiney attitudes, or taxing to-do lists—those are the things that make your family unique and distinct. And that is all any of us can bring—simply ourselves. All those moments, and all that stuff—that's what we bring to be with the Lord. He invited *you*. He wants *you* there. The Mass is for you as much as it is for each of us. Jesus wants us to come and see, to enter into worship, just as we are, seeking refuge in him, who simply wants to be with us.

Thinking and Growing as Parents

Reflect on the following questions by yourself, and then talk through your responses with your spouse, another important adult in your child's life, a good friend, or a spiritual guide.

1. What things are likely to distract you during Mass? Why do you think that is?
2. What do you typically do first when you arrive at Mass? Do you have a favorite prayer to say before Mass begins? Do you let your mind sort of wander?
3. Do you have a "four o'clock in the afternoon" moment of meeting Jesus in your life?
4. What has been helpful for you in preparing for Mass?
5. Do you remember your First Communion? What made you nervous? What were you most excited about?

Growing Together as Parents and Children

Pause a few minutes to consider all the possible teaching moments you see open up each day in your family life. What we offer in the "Growing Together as Parents and Children" sections of each chapter should be adapted for your family and home. We urge you to think of this as a "choose your own adventure" portion of the chapter. You can adapt it to use in one-on-one settings, in a school or religious-education program, or with a small group of parents or children learning and growing together.

The Mass, and receiving First Communion, can seem intimidating and complicated. There's a lot going on—lots of things to say, lots of things to do, and it can feel like a lot to remember, maneuver through, and experience fully.

When we were helping Rose prepare for her First Communion, at first we thought we needed to do sort of a "dry run" through the

Mass, stopping and explaining each little thing that was happening. We learned, rather quickly, that the "over-explain" method didn't work. Instead, when we discussed the *why* behind a specific something that was happening, and how that impacted our faith life in that very moment as well as throughout our daily lives, she was more interested, engaged, and excited.

When we stopped to have quick chats about something that confused or excited her, and related it back to moments from our lives or moments in scripture, it started to click. We hope these scripts will help start some of those conversations in your own home and with the little ones you get to walk with on the road to receiving the Eucharist for the first time.

Sample Script

Read the First Disciples story in John 1:35–42 with your child. Then work through these questions and prompts together, using the sample script to help spark conversations about what it means to "come and see" with Jesus and not be afraid to be our full, messy selves, when we do.

1. When the people in the crowd first heard John the Baptist say that Jesus was the Lamb of God, how do you think they reacted? Do you think they were interested in figuring out what that meant? Do you think they were confused? Why?
2. If you were to walk into Mass today and hear Father say, "Behold, the Lamb of God is going to sit right next to you in the pew today," what would you do? Would you run into the pew, right away, and take a seat? Would you turn around and go home? Maybe hide in the back and hope he doesn't notice you're there?

For all the comforting things we say about Jesus, we have to be honest: Jesus is kind of intimidating. He knows everything about us—our intentions, our thoughts, our hopes. He knows what we've experienced, why we've done certain things, or why we haven't. He knows us better than we even know ourselves, and when we show up to Mass with our whole messy selves, and sit down and learn that the Lord is with us, that can be kind of scary!

But Jesus knows us—he knows you and he loves you. He knows everything about you and wants to be with you. He wants you there, with him, at Mass. We go to Mass to get to know him, to be close to him. He calls us to "come and see" him, so that he can love us and remain with us. He is happy you are there and ready to be close to you. He wants you close to his heart. He wants to hear your prayers, your worries, your hopes, and even your fears.

3. Do you think Andrew and John knew that their entire lives were about to change when they talked to Jesus for the first time? Do you think they were nervous? Do you think they were excited?
4. How do you feel when you get to Mass? How do you feel about getting to receive the Eucharist for the first time? Are you excited to meet and be close to Jesus in this way?

Andrew and John are really bold and brave when they walk up to Jesus and ask him where he's staying. But they're even more brave, and more committed, when they willingly follow him that afternoon. Nothing holds them back. Even though they may have been nervous or scared, they willingly follow him.

5. Have you ever been nervous to do something new? Do you think you would have said yes to following Jesus right away? Why or why not?

Jesus *invites* Andrew and John to follow him. He doesn't force them. He doesn't make them. He doesn't trick them. Today, many hundreds of years after Jesus invited those two men to follow him, he is inviting you and me also to follow him. And remember, Jesus never forces us to follow him.

We are obligated as Catholics to go to Mass on Sundays and Holy Days of Obligation, but just simply going to Mass and being present in the church doesn't mean we are following Jesus. We could physically be in the room, in the pew, doing all the sitting, standing, and kneeling that happens in Mass, but we could still be really far from following Jesus. Instead, we have to be like Andrew and John, go over and get close to Jesus, walk beside him, talk with him, listen to him, and go with him wherever he invites us to go. Mass begins with a reminder to us that Jesus is there, saying, "Come and see." And so we should.

6. Based on what you already know about Jesus, what do you think you will see if you go and see, as Andrew and John did? What do you think Jesus will be like?

Praying as a Family

Wrap up your conversation in prayer. You might pray spontaneously, by saying aloud to the Lord whatever is on your heart and encouraging your child or the children with you to do the same. Or pray this simple prayer we offer here. Or, better yet, pray in both ways!

Lord,
Help us remember that you made us, know us, and love us.
You know what makes us nervous and excited;
you know what we struggle with and what we're proud of.
Even so, you invite us to come just as we are and see you.
Give us strength and courage not to hide from you.
Help us follow you and not hesitate when we do.
Come into the messy parts of our lives, and love us there.
Thank you for the gift of the Eucharist, which we prepare to receive.
Help us to become more like you, in all that we say and do.
Amen.

2.

Sit at the Feet of Jesus

Joining Our Stories to the Church's Story

Tommy: Color-Coded Calendars

We were drowning. Not in debt, or disastrous situations, or even from rising flood waters, though we are close to the Gulf Coast, which means hurricanes at times, and other terrible storms. Our small family of four with two children in school, multiple jobs and ministry projects to juggle, and an increasingly busy extracurricular schedule for the kids, was drowning in paper. From things appearing in the mail to flyers and newsletters coming home in our daughters' backpacks, it seemed like every time we turned around, Katie or I was trying to sort a pile of paper on a counter that had essential information or included tasks of some kind we needed to complete. It was driving us both a little crazy. With appointments and practices and meetings, as well as Katie's busy travel schedule, it was increasingly clear that we needed to find some sort of method to keep track of it all.

Blessedly, thanks to a few timely Instagram reels and a shocking realization that the phones in our pockets were useful for more than mindless scrolling, we gradually devised a shared calendar system, convinced that putting everything right into our calendars, and never letting the papers hit the counter in the first place, would keep us from drowning. With millennial ingenuity at its finest, Katie crafted a detailed color-coded system in the shared calendars, with our all-family schedule assigned green, her travel schedule colored blue, my schedule in bright orange, and pink for activities for Rose and Clare.

For a few weeks, the new system we crafted seemed to work. Katie didn't miss any scheduled interviews for her podcasts, I was on time for every school event I had to be present at, and the girls had perfect attendance at theater class. But then, the most chaotic week of the year, the week all Catholic school parents (and teachers) secretly dread, arrived. Right at the end of January, after the craziness of December and the thankfully slow return to normal routines after holiday breaks, the universe conspires to bring us Catholic Schools Week, a five-day stretch that includes dress-up days and extra school-wide events as well as a random assortment of items that need to be brought to school (but always somehow at the last minute)—all in the name of celebrating Catholic education.

We pause at this point to assure you that we are grateful for, support, have taught in, and *love* Catholic schools, of every ilk and stripe and style. We're Catholic-school believers, parents, and advocates. But Lord Almighty in the good heavens above, why must we be plagued with celebrating those schools, which we love year-round, with such gusto in one single, jam-packed week?

The brightly colored flyer outlining what our girls had to wear (and do) each day of Catholic Schools Week came home in Rose's backpack, crunched and crumpled down at the bottom. Katie, on top of our well-implemented "no papers on the counter" method, noted all the various days scheduled, put them in the corresponding calendars, and life carried on. I knew the notifications for the various days would come through when we needed them, no paper flood would drown us, and we'd be the best example of millennial-parenting productivity this side of the Mississippi. Or so I thought.

The system worked, for a little while, but then I, too busy and too distracted and too unorganized myself, sort of lost my head with the calendar. I began ignoring the notifications, silencing the calendar reminders, telling myself, *Katie will keep me posted on what I need to know,* and I fell back into a "fake it till I make it" relationship with my wife's diligently made, always notifying, shared family calendars. I'd check them when I needed to, or when I remembered to, but honestly, those calendars, as helpful as they were for a time, were beginning to make me anxious and worried about all the many things going on in our lives.

Katie: Red Shirt Rose

I was pretty proud of our color-coded calendars, if I can brag for a moment on the efficiency and simplicity of our new method. Papers didn't get piled up, things were noted in the right spot, and I even had a handle on the Catholic Schools Week dress-up days, with a notification buzzing on our phones at 5 a.m. so we knew what to put the girls in a full hour before they even woke up for the day.

And so, as the final week of January arrived—even with me traveling for the majority of the month, projects and emails piling up, and the to-do list causing more anxiety and worry than I'd care to admit—I knew the girls would get to school in the correct T-shirt, costume, or with the right craft supplies during Catholic Schools Week, all because a color-coded calendar would tell Tommy what to do. I may have been anxious and worried about work and life, but I was confident I didn't have to be when it came to home, because that calendar would save us all.

I got home late Monday night of Catholic Schools Week, my delayed flight finally landing around eleven o'clock. I promptly went to bed, with no plans to wake up any earlier than I had to after my long, frustrating day in the airport. I reset my alarm for 6:15 a.m., confident Tommy could handle morning wake-up and getting the kids dressed, just like he had for the previous few days. And when my alarm went off at 6:15, and I rolled out of bed moderately well rested, albeit still tired after long travel, I saw the notification for the Tuesday of Catholic Schools Week pop up on my phone. "Red Shirt" was on the Rose calendar, because Tuesday was patriotic day, celebrating religious liberty and the fact that Catholic schools are free and clear to operate in the United States. So Rose was going to go to school in a red shirt, because that was the simplest and easiest way to participate. No need for a flag T-shirt or a leftover Fourth of July outfit. We had a red shirt, and she was going to wear it—Catholic Schools Week conquered. I went through a quick version of my morning routine—brush teeth, fix hair, throw on a moderately put-together mom outfit—and made my way to the kitchen to say good morning to the family, hopefully finding excited little girls glad that Mommy was back and ready to head off for school.

I heard the kitchen sink as I made my way through the living room. *Must be ahead of schedule*, I thought to myself. *Tommy's already washing dishes.* An episode of *Bluey* was playing on the kitchen TV, the theme song bouncing off the walls of the house. A giggle from the girls, a bark from the dog, another buzz of a notification on my phone. All was right with the world, things were largely back to normal, and these calendars were keeping us afloat.

I stepped into the kitchen, and there, sitting at the breakfast nook, were my girls: Clare, making a pile of blueberries, wearing her play clothes for another day at daycare, and Rose in her normal plaid jumper and yellow, Peter Pan–collared, button-down shirt. I blinked twice just to make sure I was seeing it correctly, and as I went to check my phone to make sure the Rose-calendar notification had gone off for "Red Shirt," I looked over at Tommy, standing at the sink, wearing khakis and a red polo, washing the dishes without a care in the world.

"Mom, you're back!" rang out through the kitchen, and Tommy turned around from the sink, a huge smile on his face, as I stared back at him with a mixture of confusion and frustration.

"Babe? Everything okay?" he asked as he walked toward me. Clare hopped out of the breakfast nook, running to me at full speed, while Rose swiped a blueberry off her plate.

"Did you check the calendar?" I asked, forgetting even the most basic of manners in greeting my husband whom I hadn't seen in a few days.

There was only silence from Tommy, but his face began to contort as he realized I was annoyed. And I, fully aware that I really had no right to be since he'd been holding down the fort solo for a few days, dug my heels in even more. "It's red shirt day," I snapped.

"Yeah, that's why I'm in a . . . " Tommy looked down at the red shirt he was wearing, pulled the phone out of his pocket, swiped to open it, tapped over to the calendar, looked back up at me, and said, "A pink dot means Rose needs to wear a red shirt, doesn't it?" he asked sheepishly.

"I told you, Dad!" Rose cried out, "I told you it meant red shirt for me! Mom wouldn't tell *you* to wear a red shirt!" and she began to giggle.

In what can only be described as a tone of voice that required me to go to Confession later that day, I looked at my husband and snarked, "Well, it clearly doesn't matter what I do or don't tell him, because he clearly isn't using the calendar correctly if he saw 'Red Shirt' in the calendar notifications and decided to put one on himself and put you in your uniform, bud." Then I stormed out of the room through the playroom, slamming the door behind me, a crash sounding as I rushed off, annoyed at Tommy, but just as annoyed at myself for being so annoyed with him over a simple and easily fixable mistake.

He followed after me, and I fully prepared myself to pick a fight with my husband, even though I really had no right. My exhaustion and stress were coming out sideways, and I spun around on him in the hallway, ready to tell him off. "Do you not even care that I went to all that work to set up those calendars? Do you even look at them?" I whisper-shouted at him.

"I do . . . I do . . . sometimes," Tommy replied, no bite in his voice, no anger pointed back at me even though I deserved it. "They just make me a little anxious, babe. There's so much on there. It's a lot to keep straight, even with the colors and the notifications," he admitted.

And then, the wind taken out of my angry sails, we looked at each other, Tommy in his red shirt, Rose coming down the hallway trying to take off her uniform jumper so she could change into the red shirt we knew we had in the closet, and our youngest, Clare, wandering behind her, holding the cross that had fallen off the wall of the kitchen when I'd slammed the playroom door. "Momma, you knocked out Jesus!" she shouted, holding up the cross as if she were performing an exorcism on the family brawl in the hallway.

Instantly, as if a switch had been flipped for all of us, Tommy and I looked at each other and burst into laughter, collapsing onto the floor of the hallway, cackling at the absurdity of it all. And in my anger at something so silly, I had knocked out Jesus.

Rose went to her room and quickly changed, Tommy going to help her, and as I sat there continuing to giggle, Clare crawled up into my lap, handing the cross to me. I looked down at knocked-out Jesus, seeing that it was the cross I'd bought in Rome in 2013, a replica of the pectoral cross worn by Pope Francis, with the image of the Good Shepherd engraved on the front. It was my favorite image of Jesus, standing as the shepherd, with the lost sheep over his shoulders and the ninety-nine gathered behind him. My anxiety and worry and frustration began to fade as I sat there, holding Clare and sitting with the cross, waiting for Rose to emerge from the bedroom in her bright red shirt.

Learning from Scripture

Katie: A Mary Heart

Luckily, that same day, as a very busy travel stretch was winding down, I had spiritual direction scheduled. Tommy set off for work, I brought the girls to school, and then I headed back home to hop on the morning video call with the Dominican priest who often quickly, and rightly, put me in my place when I needed it.

About a half hour into our conversation and prayer, I brought up the morning fiasco with the calendars, red shirt, and falling cross, sure to emphasize that it had ended well enough with laughter, forgiveness, and a likely trip to Confession in my near future.

"You should go to Mass this evening, as a family, if you can," Father suggested. "Just hit the reset button as a family, with daily Mass. Again, if you can fit it in," he said.

It was good advice, if I'm being honest, and I felt we could all probably use some time with the Lord. It had been weeks since we'd gone to Mass as a family because I'd been on the road practically every weekend that month. "We'll try," I replied back. "But things are so busy, and I've barely been home," I muttered, secretly looking for any excuse not to give up our entire evening to 5:30 p.m. Mass on a Tuesday.

"You all might need it. Choose the better part, if you can," Father suggested gently, one more time. "Now, for your work this month, here's my suggestion, Katie…," and my spiritual director proceeded to ask me to take time to read the Gospel of Luke, chapter 10, verses 38 to 42. *Easy enough*, I thought. *Just five verses. I'll get to it tonight.*

The day unfolded, including my daily radio show, a series of extracurricular activities Tommy had to chaperone after school, and a quick trip to the store to get teacher-appreciation gifts for the last part of Catholic Schools Week. But despite my frustration at the busyness of our day, and even with the mishaps of the morning, we somehow got ourselves to daily Mass that evening. My spiritual director would be happy.

Arriving just in time to get situated in a pew in the back for the quick half hour (that would surely involve some kid gymnastics on the kneelers), I can honestly admit that I barely paid attention to what was unfolding during the Mass. I was just going through the motions: stand, sit, kneel, stand again, sit some more . . .

Mass is so familiar, and generally always more or less the same. It's almost too easy to just get into a rhythm of the same thing, over and over, following along almost mindlessly. The readings, the homily, and receiving the Eucharist are distinct and unique each time, but if we don't fully engage, actively listen, and willingly focus on the chance to be there in the first place, we can slip into an "I'm here, but I'm not *here*" mode.

We were at Mass as a family, but I wasn't really there. I was physically sitting in a pew, and I said all the things I needed to say, but my head and my heart were largely absent. Distracted by the day, still annoyed with myself at the sharp reaction to the red-shirt debacle of earlier, and now trying to keep two tiny humans moderately still for a half hour was souring my mood.

We bring our whole selves into the Mass, and the Lord wants to meet our whole selves just as we are in that space at that moment. But, just as he is present to us, we also have to be present to him. We have to fully commit to hearing the Lord speak, move, and act within the Mass. We have to be there, not just physically, but as fully engaged as we can be, sitting with the Lord, who delights in our choosing the better part—to simply be with him. Mass is our chance, sometimes the only chance we get all week, to sit still with the Lord. It's often the only place where we can rest, listen to his Word, receive his very presence within us, and then continue on with our busy lives, strengthened by the gift of the Eucharist we so desperately need and have blessedly been given.

As we got up to leave when Mass was finally over, annoyance clearly plastered across my face, Rose asked if we could go see "big Mary" in the day chapel. The statue of Our Lady Queen of Heaven had been given to the parish a few years before and set up in a small area with votive candles. Its great height (in comparison to still-petite Rose) garnered the nickname "big Mary." Tommy happily walked off with both girls, knowing I could probably use a quiet minute in the pew alone, and I suddenly remembered the other half of my homework assignment from spiritual direction.

I quickly looked up Luke 10:38–42 on my phone, pulled up the USCCB website to read the passage, and nearly threw the phone across the church when I realized what passage Father had assigned for me to read and pray with. "Martha and Mary" was at the top of the screen, a passage I'd grown to really loathe over the years, for no other reason than I think Martha is too often given a bad rap.

The interpretations of this Bible passage seem to be always more or less the same: Have a Mary heart in a Martha world. Sit still with Jesus. Listen to his words. Pay attention to what he's saying, and don't be so busy as to not notice Jesus sitting right there in front of you. Decent advice, if life isn't busy. But life is always busy, so perhaps it's actually not very good advice, and in fact patently unhelpful. Life slows down only when we are intentional enough to pump the brakes. But if you come to a screeching, grinding halt, doesn't that end up just causing a wreck?

Life *is* busy, and yet, shouldn't we find the time to meet Jesus and pay attention to him, even when it is? Can we make time for choosing the better part with the Lord and bring with us all the heavy burdens we carry in the busyness of life? Can Jesus handle our mess? If we acknowledge the busyness and noise and anxieties of our life first, and even admit our faults, can we then find the time to sit with the Lord?

Mass is precisely the place, and occasionally the only hour of the week, when we can look at the busyness of our lives, the anxieties and worries and the things that need to be jammed into color-coded calendars, and hand it all to Jesus so that we can then sit with him, try to be fully present to him, and listen to all he has to say.

The Better Part

Luke 10:38–42 is a familiar passage featuring Jesus's friends, Martha and Mary, who we also know are the sisters of Lazarus, the man Jesus will one day raise from the dead. Martha gets word Jesus is coming to visit, and probably knowing her friend's favorite foods and that he had been busy and traveling, she happily sets out a spread. The consummate host, more than willing to prepare a place for Jesus at her table, Martha is consumed with all she has to do: clean, cook, welcome guests, serve the meal, refill drinks, clean some more.

As Martha is handling all these household tasks, probably creating a system to help things go smoothly, she glances over and sees her sister, Mary, sitting with Jesus. Her sister is sitting with her friend, the friend Martha's cooked and cleaned for, the one she's hosting and serving. Martha, with her systems in place and her work underway, sees everyone else just resting and relaxing and enjoying themselves, while she herself is decidedly *not*, and she gets frustrated. Annoyed, hurt, maybe even confused as to why she's so annoyed by this, Martha marches over to Jesus and Mary and speaks her mind, asking Jesus, "Lord, do you not care that my sister has left me by myself to do the serving? Tell her to help me," she requests.

It seems simple enough—Martha is overwhelmed with everything that needs to be done, she has a system in place to do it, and she needs Mary to be looped in and help out. Jesus can make that happen. But within her request Martha reveals her heart, showing Jesus it isn't just a second pair of hands in the kitchen that she needs. Martha needs the Lord, needs his attention and his gaze, because she has made it abundantly clear that she thinks Jesus doesn't care about her. "Do you not care?" is a straightforward, passive-aggressive way of saying, "You don't care about me, Jesus, or my situation, or this burden I'm carrying, or all the work I've done, do you?"

Martha is in the presence of the Lord, who is visiting her home, and she feels completely and utterly alone. All the work she has done, all the effort she's put forth, all the plans she's made—she has set it all in motion completely by herself. She tells Jesus as much, boldly admitting that she is hurt by what's unfolding, while simultaneously deflated by the reality that she is so bothered to be doing this all on her own. Martha realizes she can't handle it all by herself. She requests help, but in admitting she needs help, she's announcing to Jesus that she feels as if he, like everyone else, doesn't see her fully.

Mary has chosen to sit with Jesus, the busyness and chaos and work of hosting Jesus entirely out of her mind. Martha has chosen to host Jesus, the ability to sit still with him and enjoy his presence utterly lost on her because she is consumed with the work that must be done. Jesus is there, with them both. Mary is consumed with listening to him. Martha is consumed with all she has to do. Mary ignores the responsibilities of the moment. Martha takes on the important responsibilities of hosting a guest. Both of them are in the presence of Jesus, but it is Martha, in this moment, who vulnerably and honestly shares exactly how she feels: unseen, unable to stop and listen, unhelped, and in some ways, unloved.

Jesus looks compassionately upon Martha, and he gently calls her attention to him. "Martha, Martha," he says. Twice he says her name. Twice he calls her to look at him. Twice he makes sure she knows he sees her. "You are anxious and worried about many things." Jesus sees her anxiety, her worry, her racing mind, and her frazzled heart. He sees the to-do list that's piled up alongside the dirty dishes. He knows she has worked all day to cook this meal. He is basking in the warmth of the home she has cleaned. He sees what she is carrying, and he names what he sees. He tells her clearly that she is not alone, because he is there, observing all she has done and is doing. He responds to her and offers her his presence fully, because she vulnerably and boldly expresses her frustration and hurt. She says what's on her mind, she shows her woundedness and hurts, and in so doing, she is met with gentle love and mercy.

Martha could have buried her frustrations and just avoided going to talk with Jesus. But instead, she went, said her piece, and so is met with peace and compassion within the Lord's own words. He sees her worries and anxieties, and he invites her to come just as she is and sit beside him, just as Mary has done. "Mary has chosen the better part," he gently tells her. The Lord acknowledges Martha's worry, sees her anxiety. And he doesn't dismiss it or tell her to get over it. He holds it within himself and invites her to sit beside him and listen to what he has to say too.

The dishes will still be dirty, and the to-do list will still be long, and the calendar notifications about school dress-up days will still ping on the phone. But Jesus is inviting each of us to set those things aside, even if just for a brief time, and to choose the better part—to sit with him and listen. In fact, Jesus invites us to bring all those things with us—the anxieties and worries and to-do lists and everything else that we're carrying—and sit down beside him. Perhaps he wants us to ask, "Do you even care?" as Martha did, because then we open ourselves fully to Jesus present with us. Only then are we vulnerable; then we can sit down, listen closely to his words and his truth, and bask in his presence.

We choose the better part and are able to listen to the Lord, but only after we've said our own piece. We find rest and sit down with Jesus, but only after we've acknowledged everything we are carrying. It is then that we can lay down our heavy burdens so that we can rest with him.

A Martha Heart

Mass begins with a greeting that reminds us of the Lord's presence. Then, in his presence, we humbly, and vulnerably, admit our faults—*grievous* faults, in fact. Three times we admit them. What a bold moment for each of us. While Martha wasn't necessarily admitting her faults by asking Jesus if he even cared about how hard she was working, she did *show* those faults and weaknesses to a certain extent. She showed her false assumptions about Mary and about Jesus, her woundedness and her hurt, her fear of being entirely alone and unseen. She spoke to Jesus out loud, in front of the entire room, in front of her own sister with whom she had a gripe. And she asked for help. It's as though she wanted to see things differently and knew that Jesus could help her do that.

When we show up to Mass just as we are—with all our sins and sorrows, with our too-busy schedules—the Church's liturgy has us do what Martha did. In full view of everyone and at full volume of our voices, we all stand up at the beginning of Mass and confess that we have messed up. And, still together, we ask the Lord for help.

Thinking and Growing as Parents

Reflect on the following questions by yourself, and then talk through your responses with your spouse, another important adult in your child's life, a good friend, or a spiritual guide.

1. What anxieties and worries pop into your head most throughout the day, or even while at Mass?
2. When have you felt most checked in or attentive at Mass? Do you remember what you did before or during the Mass to be able to pay close attention?
3. Do you feel more like Martha or Mary most days? What causes you to feel that way? Do you wish things were different in this regard? Can you change?
4. Have you experienced a time when the readings at Mass touched your heart deeply? What was the occasion and in what way(s) did the readings touch your heart? Why do you think that Mass was different for you? Is there anything you would like to do and can do to regularly experience the readings more fully?

Growing Together as Parents and Children

Read the story of Martha and Mary in Luke 10:38–42. Use the actual text from scripture, or if it would be helpful, use a children's Bible with illustrations and child-friendly language. Use whatever is helpful to hear the story and be able to discuss it. Work your way through these prompts and questions to have conversations about how we are sometimes distracted in Mass or too busy to notice Jesus wanting to sit with us.

Sample Script

Martha knew Jesus her whole life. She grew up with him. They were friends for a long time! She was so close to Jesus that she had him over to her house for dinner. And even though Jesus was her dear friend, she was still anxious about a lot of other things. Jesus was right there with her, but she was distracted and worried.

1. What do you think Martha was so worried about? What have you been worried about before?
2. How do you think Martha felt when she saw her sister, Mary, sitting at Jesus's feet? What do you think happened after she and Jesus had the conversation about her anxieties and worries?

We're worried about a lot of things sometimes, aren't we? And those worries—or distractions or responsibilities or chores or just all the stuff we have to do in life—can easily stay in our heads when we go to Mass. Our minds can wander. We can think about everything else *but* Mass, and we can rush around, sometimes not even making time to go to Mass in the first place!

3. Where does your mind drift to when you're in Mass? What do you do with all those thoughts that are bouncing around your head? What do you think Jesus would say to you when all those things are distracting you?

In every church, in every corner of the world, from the biggest basilica to the smallest country chapel, Mass is always the same. The entrance, the readings, all the sitting, standing, and kneeling—it is always the same. There's an entire formula the priest and we all follow. But most importantly, in every tabernacle in every Church throughout the world, Jesus is present. The Eucharist is there, and we can receive Jesus's Body and Blood at every Mass.

Because the Mass is always the same, sometimes we can sort of go through the motions, feel boredom creep in, and let our minds wander off to all those things that are distracting and worrying us. We can sometimes sit through an entire Mass and not even notice what we're doing!

4. Have you ever been distracted in Mass? How did that feel? Have you gotten wiggly? Or noisy? Have you needed to get up and go do something different because you're bored?

Don't feel too guilty if you get distracted. And don't feel too bad if your mind sometimes wanders or if you're consumed with all those other things you know you have to do. Jesus is still there, and he is still inviting us to sit and listen. He is still inviting us to come and see him and sit at his feet.

It's sometimes helpful to pay more attention, really listen closely, when we know what's about to happen or what to expect. The readings we hear at Mass on Sundays always follow the same pattern. There's a first reading, usually from the Old Testament (except during the Easter Season), a responsorial psalm, a second reading, which is typically from the epistles (which are letters, usually by St. Paul), and then a reading from one of the four gospels, Matthew, Mark, Luke, or John. Sometimes, for special Masses with children, we hear only one reading and the responsorial psalm before the gospel reading.

This is when we sit at the feet of Jesus, because Jesus is the Word made Flesh, dwelling among us. When we listen to God's Word in the readings at Mass, we are drawing closer to Jesus. Sometimes we feel a bit like Martha in Mass and get distracted. But hopefully, like Martha, we have the boldness and willingness to tell Jesus precisely what's going on in our heads and hearts.

Other times, we feel a bit like Mary, eager to sit at Jesus's feet and just soak it all in. Jesus wants all of us, the distracted us, the checked-in us, or the combination of the two. Because when we sit at Jesus's feet, Jesus wants to sit with us too. He wants us to hand over those distractions and worries and questions. He wants to listen to us just as we listen to him.

5. What do you want to be able to tell Jesus? What do you think you might get to hear him say to you?

Praying as a Family

Wrap up your conversation in prayer. You might pray spontaneously, by saying aloud to the Lord whatever is on your heart and encouraging your child or the children with you to do the same. Or pray this simple prayer we offer here. Or, better yet, pray in both ways!

Heavenly Father,
We come to you like Martha *and* Mary, worried about many things.
Give us the ears to hear you call our names,
and prepare our hearts to be still and listen to your words of love and life.
Keep our minds and hearts focused on you,

and when distractions come,
let us have the awareness and wisdom
to make those distractions part of our prayer.
When our minds and hearts are full of good and bad
and happy and sad and proud and anxious things,
help us hand it all over to you.
Help us sit still like Mary, and give us bold prayers like Martha.
Amen.

3.

Satisfy Your Hunger

Joining Our Stories to the Church's Story

Katie: The Ice Cream Man

"I think that's a wrap, Your Eminence," and I turned off the portable recorder that had just captured our twenty-minute conversation at the Tenth National Eucharistic Congress, which was officially beginning the next day in Indianapolis.

"That's it? I could've said more, ya know!" Cardinal Dolan chortled, his signature laugh booming out as he patted my shoulder and handed me back his microphone. "Joe, what's set for the rest of the day? Lunch?" He turned to his communications director, my immediate boss with the Archdiocese of New York and the general manager of The Catholic Channel on SiriusXM radio, for which I'd just captured the interview.

Cardinal Dolan and Joe looked at the schedule as I packed up my equipment and waited for my family to come say hello. The cardinal turned to me and asked, "Do you want to go to lunch? I hear it's your birthday!" He looked at me with a big smile and a little glint in his eye. As I was about to decline the invitation, assuming he was just being polite, my young daughters, husband, mom, and dad burst into the hotel ballroom we'd commandeered as a radio studio, and the girls ran over to say hello.

"Mommy, Daddy said we could go to Steak 'n Shake for your birthday!" Rose excitedly announced.

Clare, in her full three-year-old glory, lifted her hands in the air and belted, "Milkshakes for Mommy!" at the top of her lungs.

"There's a Steak 'n Shake?" the cardinal asked, the excitement in his voice matching that of our daughters. He turned to his crew, a quizzical look on his face, and as his priest secretary solemnly nodded and his communications director gave a thumbs-up, the smile on the cardinal's face somehow got even bigger. "Let's go get something to eat!"

I've had the privilege of being in a lot of rooms with a lot of Church leaders, bishops and otherwise, and on even the best of days I would be wildly worried about the sticky hands, loud voices, and occasional whining of my two children. We'd been traveling for a few days at this point, and I knew my girls were, at times, just tapped out from sitting still, listening quietly, or even just eating with very basic manners. Restaurants on a good day are a considerable amount of effort for most young families, and a restaurant with the cardinal archbishop of New York, who also happens to be my boss, was, I thought, a fiasco waiting to happen.

But as we walked to the restaurant, traversing the streets of downtown Indianapolis, and Cardinal Dolan visited with my family, making jokes with six-year-old Rose and pushing three-year-old Clare's stroller, I couldn't help but think, *This, truly, is the Church.* My mom and dad, married for more than forty years, were walking alongside a cardinal, now ordained for more than forty years. My two little girls, their wiggly wonderful selves, were chatting up this high-ranking Church official as if they were longtime friends with him.

Along the way, we ran into a group of young adults who had spent the previous two months walking from Connecticut to Indianapolis as part of a Eucharistic pilgrimage. The cardinal invited them to join us for lunch, and by the time we arrived at the Steak 'n Shake, we were a group of twelve. "Whatever you want, folks," the cardinal declared as we began to order. "My treat!"

When the burgers and shakes were brought to our pushed-together tables, the whole restaurant sang "Happy Birthday" to me, led by Cardinal Dolan. I blushed and thanked everyone and then turned to Clare to help her dip her French fries in ketchup. I had noticed her staring at the cardinal, and she seemed enamored with everything about him, from the shiny cross around his neck to his loud and jovial laugh, which she matched quickly with her high-pitched giggles. Clare and the cardinal were two peas in a pod and fast friends. She'd look at him, he'd wink at her, she'd reach for his pectoral cross, he'd tickle her chin. It was like watching magnets, a seventy-four-year-old prince of the Church and an almost-four-year-old girl, somehow instant best buddies.

"What do I call you?" Clare curiously asked the cardinal. She'd heard me say "Eminence" a handful of times, and I realized she probably thought that was his name, not just the formal title one uses to address a cardinal.

"Well . . . " he began. "My nieces and nephews call me Uncle Tim. Most everyone else just calls me Cardinal Dolan. I used to be Fr. Tim, and then Bishop Dolan, and then Archbishop Dolan." He looked off in the distance for a moment, as if his nearly fifty years of priesthood were flashing before his eyes as he recalled his various titles and names.

Clare just stared at him, as if she found his answer lacking, and said only, "Huh."

Cardinal Dolan smiled, realizing she was probably confused, and reached over to his vanilla milkshake, pulled the straw out, and passed it over to Clare. "How about you just call me the ice cream man?" He chuckled as he handed the whipped-cream-covered straw to my three-year-old, who grabbed it immediately and shoved it into her own milkshake, now the proud owner of two straws, both given to her by a man who votes for the pope.

Cardinal Dolan and I smiled at each other, a tender moment shared between a prince of the Church and a mom who works for him hosting daily Catholic radio. "You're doing good, kid," the cardinal affectionately said, patting me on the back as we launched into a conversation about the Eucharistic Congress, which had brought all of us to Indianapolis.

Just as he began asking me what my role would be in the coming days, Clare reached over, hands sticky from her lunch and milkshake, and tapped the cardinal on the arm. "You're gonna be *Uncle* Dolan," she announced.

"Not the ice cream man?" he asked back, winking at her as she stared him down.

"Noooo!" she laughed. "You're Uncle Dolan!" Clare broke out into a giggle, sparking laughter across the whole table, before she turned back to Cardinal Dolan, looked him square in the eye, and said, "You're my Uncle Dolan and you feed me."

Cardinal Dolan and his crew said their goodbyes and left the Steak 'n Shake a bit before we did. Our slow-moving gang had to wash hands and faces after the myriad milkshakes with whipped cream. But when we did finally walk out of the restaurant, Joe, the cardinal's communications director, ducked back in, walked up to the self-order kiosk, and ordered five meals of burgers and fries. "Still hungry, Joe?" I joked as we walked by him.

He turned and smiled, beckoned me over, and whispered, "Cardinal sent me back in to buy a few meals for some of the homeless men around the corner. He just wanted to give them something to eat too."

Tommy: "He Feeds Me"

Early the next morning, as we were getting the girls ready for a very full day that would include seeing their mom host a morning session of the Eucharistic Congress in an NFL stadium, Katie couldn't stop gushing about all of us eating lunch with Cardinal Dolan the day before. All too aware of how full his schedule is, she was tickled that he'd taken the time to be with us, visit with the girls, and get to know her parents. She had known him from work and hosting radio. Now he knew us and our family in a more personal way.

As Katie was braiding the girls' hair, I heard her say, "Y'all are very lucky the cardinal took us out to lunch. Not everyone gets to do that, ya know."

Just as Rose began asking why cardinals are so busy and what they have to do every day, Clare piped up. "Well, he's Uncle Dolan, so of course he gives us food."

"*Cardinal* Dolan, Bear," Katie gently corrected. "We call him *Cardinal*. Or Your Eminence. That's the correct title, and we want to be respectful."

"Well, he's *my* Uncle Dolan," Clare said matter-of-factly, walking out of the bathroom with half her hair braided, announcing she was ready to go to breakfast. "He feeds me, so he's Uncle Dolan."

Out of the room, down the hall, and into the elevator of the Westin Hotel in downtown Indianapolis, Katie breathed a sigh of relief when no one else joined our motley crew to ride down to the lobby. We'd been placed at the same hotel as the majority of the bishops and cardinals in attendance at the Eucharistic Congress, and my wife was trying hard to ensure that the girls were polite and quiet when encountering the mitered men wearing large crosses. After a quick ride down, we walked into the lobby, where we were immediately greeted by the Church on full display. Priests and religious sisters, bishops, cardinals, and laypeople were all chatting and sharing a few moments over coffee and croissants before the rush of the day.

As Katie's folks drifted over to some of the sisters to say good morning, I told her to go say a quick hello to Cardinals Tagle and Pierre, both of whom she'd gotten to know during the Synod on Young People a few years before. Hesitant, not wanting to leave me alone with both girls in the sea of people, I assured her we'd be fine for the two minutes she'd be chatting with them. But just as Katie stepped away, with lightning-fast fingers and nothing but pure determination, Clare unbuckled herself from the stroller and bolted over to Cardinal Dolan, who was seated nearby chatting with some other clergymen.

"Uncle Dolan!" Clare shouted as she jumped up onto the couch next to him, wrapping her little arms around him as he looked down, surprised to see her.

"Clare Bear!" he bellowed happily. "Good morning!" And he hugged her back.

I saw Katie quickly step away from the cardinals and heard her say, "Excuse me, Your Eminences, but my youngest is . . . ," and she gestured over to Clare, who had made herself quite cozy next to Cardinal Dolan, chatting him up as if he were an old college pal she had not seen in years. I saw the two cardinals smile as Katie rushed over, me still pushing the now-empty stroller while Rose walked over to the Sisters of Life, whom she knew well, to hug them good morning.

"Clare, we've got to go get breakfast," Katie said as she stepped into the little sitting area, trying to extract our daughter from the gaggle of priests and bishops, a sheepish look on her face as she went to make a quick apology for the disruption.

"Uncle Dolan already gave me something to eat," Clare said, her mouth full of croissant as Cardinal Dolan beamed beside her, the croissant he'd been eating ripped in half, part of it now being chewed by our daughter, the rest clutched tightly in her little hand.

The few people sitting there began to laugh at her quick response to her mother, and while Katie stood there uneasy, Cardinal Dolan chortled, "Steak 'n Shake. Bread. What's next? You want to receive First Communion this morning, too, Clare?"

Without missing a beat, Clare looked up at the cardinal archbishop of New York, hopped off the couch, wiped her crumb-covered hands on his sleeve, and said, "Yes! I want *you* to give me Jesus, Uncle Dolan."

The people in earshot seemed clearly surprised at what Clare had just said, giving voice to her fairly well-articulated comprehension of the Eucharist. "And then, more ice cream!" she added. Everyone erupted in laughter, and Clare hugged Cardinal Dolan again before hopping off the couch, going back to her stroller, and informing me she was ready for real breakfast and it was time to go.

Two hours later, after *real* breakfast at a diner and a quick walk down to Lucas Oil Stadium for the opening Mass of the Eucharistic Congress, we settled into our seats. Within a short while, Cardinal Dolan prayed the Eucharistic Prayer, saying, "This is my Body, which will be given up for you," and he elevated the host in a stadium full of nearly fifty thousand people. Clare leaned over just then and whispered in my ear as she pointed down from section 214, "See, Daddy, Uncle Dolan is giving us something to eat!"

Learning from Scripture

Give Them Some Food

It may sound simplistic, but we go to Mass to get something to eat. Whether for the thousandth time or the very first time, we are there for a meal. We are there to consume something of inestimable value. We are at Mass to feast, hopefully as excited to receive the Eucharist as would be a three-year-old to go get burgers and milkshakes, have a morning croissant, or enjoy real breakfast.

Mass should never be a fast-food, drive-thru meal, nor one eaten hastily to simply take in calories and keep our bodies functioning. While busy lives may necessitate eating this way often, the Eucharistic banquet is meant to be carefully orchestrated, slowly digested, joyful, and deeply satisfying. It feeds our souls. It forms us—week after week—into a people who love one another and are sent to make the world somehow better, for everyone. The Eucharistic banquet in which we participate each Sunday (and sometimes between Sundays) makes us the Body of Christ once more.

The gospels give us wonderful stories of Jesus eating—popping into homes, sitting down with his disciples for a quick bite, attending feasts where the wine runs low and suddenly is miraculously replenished. Meals meant something to Jesus, and it is within the context of a final meal with his disciples that he gave us the Eucharist. But even in the spontaneous, thrown-together meals, Jesus reveals deep truths that will satisfy our hunger.

After the apostles were sent out to do the mighty works they'd seen Jesus himself do—healing and preaching and proclaiming God's kingdom—they returned to Jesus to reconnect and process all that occurred. This ragtag group of men called together by Jesus to follow him and change the world returned to be by his side to rest at Jesus's feet and be still with him.

It's in that stillness, where Jesus and his closest followers sought solitude, that a great crowd begins to gather, eager to see who Jesus was. Five thousand men plus many women and children gather to listen to him. We can imagine them hanging on his every word and whispering to one another about what he might mean. These are the words of the one who sends his apostles to preach and heal, the words of the one who casts out demons and brings sight to the blind. These are people eager to listen, hungry for a saving message, and Jesus is moved by them.

Matthew (14:13–21) and Mark (6:34–44) both note that Jesus is so moved with pity for this crowd that he cures the sick and lets the crowds stay long past the day's end. Luke (9:10–17) says that Jesus receives the crowd of people and preaches about the kingdom of God. John (6:1–15) notes that Jesus sees the crowd and asks Philip about the dinner plans. Evening is falling, and the people are not leaving. The logistics, and potential problems, of a crowd of that size gathered in a deserted place begins to set in.

The apostles are worried about how they are to feed so very many people. There were no Holy Land food trucks waiting around the corner. There were no delivery options. In their worry they go to Jesus with a plan: Send the crowds away. They can't be responsible for that much food for that many people. No one will be bothered by an end to this hastily thrown-together event, and surely this is the right solution: Everyone goes home. But all four gospels say that Jesus tells his followers to give them something to eat. And despite their quick protests, concerns about how much this would cost (two hundred days' wages), and their realization that the only food on site is five loaves and two fish, Jesus insists they can fix this hunger problem. He can feed them. Right there. Right then. With what he has right in front of him.

This seems entirely impossible, of course—unreasonable, and even maybe a little ridiculous. Five loaves. Two fish. Five thousand people. The math just ain't mathing, Lord! And yet, the apostles do as Jesus instructs. When Jesus looks to the heavens, gives thanks, blesses and then breaks the bread, he first gives it to his disciples. They see the miracle with their own eyes—this miracle of multiplication. Jesus feeds them and then sends them out into the crowd to feed the multitudes. The doubters, the worriers, the first followers of Jesus who themselves had gone out to preach and heal, are reminded that Jesus provides.

In these different versions of the same story, we can learn an essential truth: Jesus wants to feed us, caring for us in our most basic needs. Jesus compassionately, joyfully, and miraculously feeds the crowd gathered to listen at his feet. He doesn't just feed them with his words; he feeds them with food. He provides a meal that seems to come from nowhere, and yet is enough to feed everyone and have leftovers. This is the same Lord we meet each time we go to Mass.

An Exchange of Love

When we arrive at church for Mass, we settle into our own quiet, out-of-the way place, and we, like those first followers of Jesus, wait for him. Hopefully, we are ready to listen and learn and be fed by him. Jesus gazes upon us and receives all that we offer to him, whatever we have right then, right there. Sometimes this is only our broken, tired, chaotic selves. And at other times, it is our exuberant, eager, grateful selves. But no matter who we are or what we have to offer him at any given Mass, we are asked to enter into an exchange of love. We give ourselves to Christ, and he gives to us himself wholly and completely in the bread and wine made Christ's Body and Blood. We receive him in Holy Communion, and we say, "Amen!"

The Eucharistic exchange of love isn't a magic trick, it isn't a symbol, and it isn't just play-acting some ancient ritual documented in an old book—the Eucharist is a miracle, each and every time. We get to be present there and partake of Christ, receiving him into our own bodies. And then we are sent into the world to proclaim this miracle by our love of and care for all whom we encounter.

That's Really Jesus?

We took Rose to Eucharistic Adoration a few weeks before her First Communion. This is a devotional practice of quiet prayer and meditation before the tabernacle, where the Blessed Sacrament is reserved. While we were settling in, I whispered the very same thing we say every time we drive past the Church on our way to school, "Hi, Jesus." Rose turned to me, shock on her little face, and whisper-shouted, "Mom, *that's really Jesus?*" as she pointed furiously at the monstrance holding the consecrated host in the perpetual adoration chapel.

"Uh, yes. It's always been Jesus. Who did you think it was?" I gently whispered back. Suffice it to say, we had to step out of the chapel a few moments later so we could continue the conversation and not disturb others, because here we were, just a few weeks shy of First Communion, and the mysterious miracle of the Eucharist was, as it so often is, puzzling. My daughter, as do we all, needed to think this through again.

"It's really Jesus?" "Yes, Bud."

"Not just like a reminder of Jesus?" "Nope, really Jesus."

"But why?" "Because he loves us."

"But enough to do that?" "Do what?"

"Become bread!" "Well, the bread becomes him."

"But it's bread!*"* "Not anymore. . . . Now it's Jesus."

"But bread is so . . . " "Boring?"

"It's bread! It's nothing special!" "And yet, that's precisely how Jesus comes to us. Humble and small and simple."

"And it's really him, Mom?" "Yes, it's really him, Rose."

"And he wants me *to receive him?"* "It's the only thing he wants, yes."

"*You're sure?"* "I'm sure."

"It's Jesus?" "It's Jesus."

Whether you're a seven-year-old a few weeks out from First Communion baffled by the theological realities of the Eucharist, or an adult who has never made much sense of the Eucharist at any point in your life, it's Christ Jesus, Our Lord, present to us in the Eucharist. Whether you're a pious attendee of daily Mass, or it's been a really long time since you even darkened the doorstep of a Catholic church, much less gone inside to receive the Eucharist, it's really Christ Jesus. Whether you're a cradle Catholic, a converted Catholic, a lapsed Catholic, a doubting Catholic, a Catholic hater, a confused Catholic, a quiet or loud or joyful or sometimes mopey Catholic, wherever you fall on the spectrum of receiving in the hand or the tongue, wearing chapel veils or flip-flops, liking Latin or liturgical dance, in every tabernacle in every church around the world, and at every Mass when Father prays, "This is my Body, which will be given up for you," it is really Christ Jesus, present with us and for us.

And the Eucharist is not just here to look at, think about, discuss, or even wave hello to on the drive to school each morning. We adore the Eucharist, praising God from whom all blessings flow. But first and foremost, the Eucharist is food. Mass is a meal. And Jesus, truly present, feeds us.

Thinking and Growing as Parents

Read one of the biblical accounts of the Feeding of the Five Thousand, found in Matthew 14:13–21, Mark 6:30–44, Luke 9:10–17, or John 6:1–15 (here known as the story of the Multiplication of the Loaves). If time allows and you're curious, read all four, and pay attention to some of the subtle differences in each recounting of the miracle. Also, note the similarities. After reading, reflect on the following questions by yourself, and then talk through your responses with your spouse, another important adult in your child's life, a good friend, or a spiritual guide.

1. What's your favorite meal? To cook? To eat? To share? What's special about it? Why do you like having it? With whom do you like sharing it?
2. What do you remember most about being prepared for your own First Communion? Did it involve conversations about the Eucharist as a sacred meal in which we partake of the Body and Blood of Christ? How do you understand this teaching today?
3. Is there anything particularly confusing, or even frustrating, about the Church's teachings on the Eucharist? What do you feel like you yourself need to pray or learn more about?
4. When you go to Mass, what stands out to you the most? What confuses you the most?
5. Do you feel *fed* at Mass? If so, why? If not, why not? Does going to Mass feel like a chance to be fed by Jesus?

Growing Together as Parents and Children

Thinking about the Feeding of the Five Thousand, reflect on the ways Jesus remains concerned for the well-being of the crowd and insists that the people not be sent away. Jesus wants to feed them, and he does. Use the following questions and prompts to talk about the exchange of love this story represents and the one that we participate in during Mass as we give ourselves to Jesus and he gives himself to us.

Sample Script

There is a Bible story usually called the Feeding of the Five Thousand, and in the Gospel of John it is called the Multiplication of the Loaves. It's the only miracle, besides the Resurrection of Jesus, that we find in all four gospels. That's how important the story is! You probably know most of the details, don't you? There's a hungry crowd, some worried apostles, a super calm Jesus, and a few loaves and fish. Let's listen to one version of the story now.

Choose one of the gospel readings cited above, and read it aloud. Or have your child read it aloud.

1. How do you think that little boy felt when the apostles asked him if they could take his five loaves and two fish? Before the apostles even went over to talk to him, how do you think they felt?
2. Jesus seems very calm and unbothered by the fact that there are so many people that are so hungry. Why do you think he was so calm? Do you think he always knew what he was going to do?
3. The feeding of more than five thousand people is a miracle in three ways. First, it's a miracle of *multiplication*. The hungry people are fed with just a little bit of food. Jesus takes a little, and he makes a lot more. Second, it's a miracle of *trust*. The apostles had to trust that Jesus knew what he was doing and that he could provide for them and everyone else. And third, it's a miracle of *abundance*. There is more than enough food as soon as Jesus begins to bless, break, and distribute the bread. There are even leftovers! Jesus multiplies. Jesus proves his power. Jesus provides abundantly.

The same thing happens when we go to Mass. Jesus provides for us and shows us his goodness by coming to us in the Eucharist. He multiplies grace in our lives, bringing us closer and closer to him when we receive his Body and Blood in Holy Communion.

4. When we go to Mass, we are experiencing a miracle, just like those people experienced when they gathered together in the gospel story to listen to Jesus. Does it feel like that to you? Does Mass feel like a miracle?

5. When you think about receiving Communion for the very first time, what are you most excited about? What are you most nervous about? Do you really believe that Jesus will feed you?

On that day, when five thousand people are fed, the apostles are worried, Jesus is at peace, the crowd is excited—there are so many feelings, so much going on. But Jesus provides, and everyone eats to their fill. What seems like a very desperate situation, something the apostles seem annoyed by, ends up being a miraculous moment that's documented in all four gospels!

6. Have you ever been worried Jesus won't be able to provide for you? How has that felt? When you think about receiving First Communion, does it feel like Jesus will be giving something to fill you up?
7. Jesus provides for us in so many ways. It isn't always just a meal, as when he fed all those people, or even limited by his coming to us in Holy Communion. Jesus feeds us with truth, with goodness, with beauty, with grace. He sees what we need and takes care of us. Have you ever asked Jesus to provide something for you? To give you something? What was it, and why did you want it?

When we go to Mass, we go hungry. Maybe we are not always physically hungry, but certainly we are spiritually hungry because we want to be close to Jesus. So, we go to hear God's Word in the readings and to listen carefully to what the priest or deacon preaches about. We go to give ourselves to Jesus and to receive him in return, by taking and eating, taking and drinking, Holy Communion.

When we step forward to receive Communion, we are consuming what Jesus has provided for us—his whole self. He feeds us just like he fed those people all those years ago on the hillside. Just as regular food nourishes us, in Holy Communion Jesus nourishes us with his very self. What was just bread is no longer just bread. And the wine is no longer just wine. Jesus is now there. And in the same way that the Feeding of the Five Thousand was a miracle of multiplication, trust, and abundance, the Eucharist is a miracle. The grace of God is multiplied in our hearts. We place our trust in Jesus to be with us always, and because of Holy Communion, we are abundantly blessed.

8. What is your favorite meal? Why do you like eating it so much? Is it a favorite food you get to have with your family, or maybe out at

a favorite restaurant? Is it something Mom or Dad cooks only on special occasions? Why is it so tasty? Why is it your favorite?

We love to eat our favorite meal because we know it tastes good, it usually has some good memories associated with it, and it fills us up and brings us joy. The Eucharist isn't just a regular meal but a *spiritual* meal that we get to consume physically when we take and eat, take and drink, Holy Communion.

9. What are you most excited about for your First Communion? Why? Do you have any questions about this spiritual meal and this beautiful gift of the Eucharist?

Praying as a Family

Wrap up your conversation in prayer. You might pray spontaneously, by saying aloud to the Lord whatever is on your heart and encouraging your child or the children with you to do the same. Or pray this simple prayer we offer here. Or, better yet, pray in both ways!

Jesus, you are the source of all goodness and life.
You don't just give a little; you give a lot.
You feed us with your very Body and Blood.
Give us the courage to receive the good gifts you give us,
to trust you, and to love you more and more.
Help us to believe in the Eucharist, love the Eucharist,
and receive the Eucharist worthily and with great trust and joy.
Feed us, Lord, and fill us up.
Amen.

4.

Only Say the Word

Joining Our Stories to the Church's Story

Katie: What's the Word?

"Katie, it's time to go! We can't be late!" came the shout across the offices of Terranova and Prejean, Certified Public Accountants. My mom was right. We would be late if we didn't leave within the next five minutes, and so my sixth-grade self packed up her backpack—the rolling kind with spinny wheels, which were all the rage just then—and rushed downstairs to load up our Suburban and head down Lake Street to church for daily Mass.

If we didn't leave by 4:50, we'd get caught in the surge of traffic that magically appeared at 4:55, and then we'd be rolling in by the skin of our teeth for 5:30 Mass, for which I was the assigned altar server, three days a week. Reluctantly, I should add. I'd enjoyed the altar serving at first. There was something beautiful about being able to see what was happening at the altar up close, as well as being able to help Father with all the little things that had to be done, such as the hand washing and the table setting.

But, as with many things for little kids, it lost its luster quickly, especially when I'd been asked if I could be the regular altar server for the evening Mass every Monday, Wednesday, and Friday. I told my mom I wanted to join the choir with my violin. She said we could do both. I did not win the argument, and so here was another Friday that would not become the weekend until after that evening Mass, making me late for a sleepover at Mary Beth's house. Again.

I grudgingly walked into the sacristy that afternoon, my mom trailing behind me to help get things set up for the extraordinary ministers of Holy Communion, for whom she served as captain at the—you guessed it—Monday, Wednesday, and Friday 5:30 evening Masses. Laura, my younger sister, who was only in second grade, went and sat on a chair by the door that led out into the main church, her nose buried in a book, as it usually was.

Msgr. Groth came barreling into the sacristy at 5:15, sweat glistening on his wrinkled forehead. He had silver white hair, the smoothest skin I'd ever seen on anyone's face, and very white teeth. It's funny what I remember about the priests of my childhood. Msgr. Ronnie Groth was like the beardless, younger brother of Santa Claus to me.

"I need more priests to hear Confessions more often! Too many sinners these days!" he joked as he whipped open his vestments closet and grabbed the green stole and chasuble hanging in front of a full-length mirror. "Wrinkled! Again!" Monsignor complained a lot, but always with a happy tone and never with a grumble. He was, if a jokester, quick with a compliment, self-deprecating and funny, and a good homilist who made attending daily Mass three times a week at least tolerable for my "I'm tired of this" self. I liked Msgr. Groth, and he was always very kind to me.

He got himself vested. "There, I'm recombobulated," he'd say nearly every day, and then he turned to me, sitting on the little brown chair by the confessional door, in my off-white alb with the processional cross leaned against the wall beside me. "Ah . . . there she is. Sister Mary Kathryn Elizabeth of the Seven Wounds of Christ. And how are we today?"

This was his signature line, always accompanied with a little wink. Msgr. Groth allowed female altar servers at the parish because he was convinced it would revive young women entering religious communities and becoming nuns, and he never failed to give us sister names and suggest communities to go visit. I'd been told to visit the Dominicans in Nashville every week for a year. He'd tell the young men that they'd look good in a collar, and he'd even hold his tab collar up to their necks from time to time to give them a quick feel for the priestly life.

Before I could tell him how my day was, or that I had a sleepover at my best friend's house that night, hoping he'd catch the hint that I'd like a short homily, he startled. "Oh, and who do we have here? Laura, what are you doing here?" Totally overlooked by the both of us, my little sister, who was quite petite as a second grader, was still sitting on a chair by the door next to the steps that led into the main church. Her book was now closed, her eyes trained on Monsignor and me as we both noticed her for the first time.

"Mom was talking to Dr. Ordinario. She told me to sit right here and wait, so I did."

"Ah, no problem! Do you want to serve, too, Sister Laura Marie Scholastica of the Sacred Heart of Jesus?" Msgr. Groth could've named a whole convent if he'd been given the chance.

"Can't. Too little," Laura quickly replied.

"Nonsense. We have albs short enough for you," Monsignor retorted, turning to the other set of closets full of the albs and cassocks used by children of varying sizes.

"No, I haven't made my First Communion yet. So I can't," Laura said back, a slight edge to her little voice, as if annoyed that the pastor of our parish didn't realize she was coming up for a blessing and not receiving the Eucharist three times a week at Mass.

"Ah. Well, then call me next year, how about?" Monsignor joked back, phased not at all by the tiny sarcastic child sitting in his sacristy. "Sister Katie, shall we?"

He turned to me, but then Laura spoke up again. "Monsignor, can I ask you a question?" Laura asked.

"Make it quick, if you can," our pastor smiled back, glancing down at his watch. "We only have a few minutes, and Katie here has plans, I can tell, so this will be a fast Mass if I can make it one," and he glanced back over at me and winked again.

"Msgr. Groth," Laura stood up from the chair, straightened her spine, and looked him squarely in the eye. It was like a strange standoff about to unfold, my tiny little sister standing across from our big-bellied pastor with bright white hair and even whiter teeth. "What's the word?" Laura asked.

"Excuse me, dear?" Monsignor asked. "What word?" He turned toward the table that had the Roman Missal (the book with the prayers for Mass that the priest uses throughout) and fiddled with the ribbons as he opened it to glance down at the pages.

"The 'only say the word' word," Laura quipped back. "What's *that* word?"

"Hmm?" Monsignor was distracted now, flipping through the Missal that he would carry in during the procession for daily Mass, insisting he carry it himself, under his arm like the newspaper, because, "It's *my* guidebook, after all. I'd be lost without it!" This was another of his signature phrases.

"'Only say the word and I shall be healed.' We say that at Mass. What's the word to heal us, Monsignor?"

Slowly, as if suddenly surprised by the inquiry from my second-grade sister, Msgr. Groth turned toward Laura standing there, finally fully noticing her from her plaid Catholic-school jumper to the book she was holding in her hand, a children's missal my mom had bought her at the Catholic bookstore just the week before.

"What's the word?" Monsignor parroted back to her.

"What's the word?" Laura asked again.

"I don't think anyone's ever asked me that," he murmured to himself. And then, startled again by the bells' sudden ringing, signaling it was half past the hour, Monsignor turned to Laura and said, "Are you shy?"

"Uh . . . " She turned bright red, her mild-mannered, somewhat shy self now suddenly embarrassed by her brief moment of brave inquiry moments before.

"Never mind, just sit with your mom during Mass, and be ready, Sister Laura," Monsignor said. "Sister Katie of the Seven Wounds, it's showtime!"

Ten minutes later, Msgr. Groth began his homily with a big smile on his face. "I say Mass every day, and talk to people every day, and see these Prejean girls at Mass nearly every day. One of them is bound to be a nun, right, Marie?" and he turned to smile at my mom sitting with my little sister beside her.

"Today, for the first time ever, someone asked me a question I'm not sure I've ever been asked before," Monsignor continued. "Laura, come up here." With a little cajoling, my sister made her way to the front of the church, and Monsignor pulled her into the sanctuary to stand beside him as he preached. This little girl asked me the best question I've ever been asked, proving to me that we all need to pay a little more attention at Mass." He looked down at Laura and said, "Do you want to tell them what you asked me, Laura?"

He unclipped his mic from the collar of his chasuble and held it down to Laura, who said, with a trembling voice, "I asked you what the one word is."

"You did indeed!" Msgr. Groth bellowed. "She asked me what the word is. And you know what? You probably don't even know what word Laura means, do you? She's talking about the moment when we say, 'Only say the word and I shall be healed,' right before we receive Communion. *That* word. She's paying such close attention! She wants to know the one word!"

Msgr. Groth thanked Laura for coming forward, sent her back to the pew with my mom, and proceeded to launch into a homily about being attentive and checked in at Mass, even a daily Mass you go to often where it's easy to just go through the motions and not notice what's happening. It was a lovely homily, one that I remember much about to this day, decades later.

But after Mass, as we drove home, while Mom gushed from the driver's seat about how Laura had impressed Msgr. Groth with her very thoughtful question, Laura leaned over to me and whispered, "He didn't answer my question, Katie. I still don't know what that word is."

"The Word Is Amen"

I never forgot that Friday evening Mass. We often joked about the time Laura got called up during the homily because she'd stumped the priest, who never did answer her question, as she was quick to remind us. We'd laugh at the realization that it probably set her on her career path, leading her to become a doctor of canon law (Church law) and a religious: Sister Lilianna Petra, of the Sisters of Life, I'm sure much to the heavenly delight of now-deceased Msgr. Groth. But above all, the moment has stuck with me because my sister was, at just seven years old, attentive to something happening in Mass that confused her, and she sought an answer (even if she never did really get it at the time).

It should be duly noted that, yes, in all her theological study and now in religious life, Laura certainly knows what "the word" is. She knows that the words "Lord, I am not worthy that you should enter under my roof, but only say the word and my soul shall be healed" come from the story of Jesus's healing of a Roman centurion's servant in the Gospel of Matthew (8:5–13). The words are spoken by the centurion who longs for the healing of his servant and shows profound trust that Jesus can bring that healing, simply by "saying the word."

My sister eventually learned the answer she sought from our pastor all those years ago, and we still tell the story frequently in our family—most recently at her final home visit the June before she entered a new stage in her formation with the Sisters of Life. Gathered around the dining-room table in our childhood home, laughing about all the moments we probably should've noticed that Laura would be the nun in the family, we tried to remember all the various sister names Msgr. Groth had given us over the years, and we told the tale of little Laura stumping Monsignor with a question that maybe only a future canon lawyer would think to ask.

Rose, Laura's goddaughter, sat beside my sister as we told the story. Rose leaned against Laura's arm, soaking in every second she could with her Wawa—a nickname given when Rose was little and couldn't say *L*'s yet. Wawa looked down at Rose and asked, "Do you want to come to daily Mass with me tomorrow?"

A fresh First Communicant, anxious to receive the Eucharist any chance she could, Rose immediately nodded yes. A few minutes later, as she trotted off to bed, the promise of some one-on-one time with Wawa giving a bounce to her step, Rose turned around to all of us at the table and said, "Wawa, what *is* the word, by the way?"

"What, bud?" Laura replied absent-mindedly, only half paying attention.

"The word? That priest didn't answer your question, but do you know now?" We all chuckled, marveling at the fact that Rose, as always, was half listening to the conversation we were having at the table. Sharp ears on that kid!

"The word . . . Well, it isn't just *one single* word," Laura began.

But just as she was gearing up for what would likely be a hefty explanation, putting all her theological study to good use, Rose quipped back, "It's *Amen*, Wawa. The word is *Amen*. Everyone in second grade knows that. Do you know that word, Wawa? *Amen* is the one word."

Learning from Scripture

Lord, I Am Not Worthy, but Only Say the Word

In the final moments of the Liturgy of the Eucharist, after the host has been consecrated and we have prayed the Our Father and offered each other a sign of peace, just before we go to Communion, we proclaim what the Lamb of God has done for us and for all of creation. The Lamb of God, Jesus, has taken away the sins of the world, and so we ask for his mercy and peace. Salvation is possible because of Christ Jesus, who gave his life on our behalf. Mercy and peace will make salvation ever more real for each of us if we but remain close to Jesus.

We kneel back down, and after a brief moment of quiet, the priest holds up the consecrated bread and wine, physical things perceptible to our senses and also sacred signs that point us to the deeper reality of Christ Jesus, who is present there. When the Church tells us that we receive the Body and Blood of Christ in Holy Communion, she means that Christ comes to us physically—and we call this physical presence "the Body and Blood of Christ." This language we use at Mass originates from Bible stories of the Last Supper, which you can read in 1 Corinthians 11:23–25 and in the Gospels of Matthew 26:17–24, Mark 14:12–25, and Luke 22:7–38. We encourage you to read these, right now if you can.

As we kneel at Mass, just before Communion, eyes fixed on the Blessed Sacrament—the Body and Blood of Christ—held high by the priest for all of us to see, we hear him repeat the message of John the Baptist from the Gospel of John (1:29): "Behold, the Lamb of God, who takes away the sins of the world." And we are called to the Eucharistic banquet, the joyous feast of the Lamb of God (see Revelation 19:9).

How very good it is to be there! After all our listening, all our praying, and all our participating through the opening rites of Mass, the Liturgy of the Word (when we hear the scriptures proclaimed and a homily preached for us), and the Eucharistic Prayer, we now arrive at the moment when we are to receive Christ in Holy Communion.

In anticipation of this great gift, we humble ourselves before our Eucharistic Lord and, on our knees, we echo the Roman centurion whom we talked about earlier in this chapter. In the gospel story, Jesus tells the centurion that he will go cure the servant, to which the centurion replies, "Lord, I am not worthy to have you enter under my roof; only say the word and my servant will be healed" (Matthew 8:8). Sound familiar?

As a small child, my sister homed in on the "word" in this proclamation of faith, thinking it was one single word that would boom down from the heavens. A single word that would fix all the problems, heal all the wounded souls, and put things back into right order. Perhaps the centurion who first made this declaration millennia ago thought the same.

Jesus's reputation precedes him at this point in the gospels. He has healed and preached. He has challenged authorities and flipped established customs and laws and teachings on their head. He has gathered his apostles and begun to travel. When he arrives in Capernaum, a centurion comes up to him—a Gentile, not a Jew, someone who isn't necessarily looking for the Messiah. An authority within the Roman military, this centurion soldier who wields power himself is desperate. His power means very little in the face of an illness he cannot fix. Concerned for his servant who is sick at his home, the centurion approaches Jesus with a request: "Lord, my servant is lying at home paralyzed, suffering dreadfully" (Matthew 8:6).

No greeting, no introduction of himself, no casual chitchat with offers of an easier time for Jesus if he just gives the centurion what he wants—this is a desperate man, who feels there's no hope, unless Jesus can intervene.

Only Say the Word

Jesus is moved by the centurion's request. In Luke's account of the miracle, Jesus learns this is a man who has been friendly to the Jews, helping build their synagogue and places of worship. But in Matthew's account, Jesus doesn't have to be convinced or given more details. "I will come and cure him" (Matthew 8:7), Jesus says, and as he prepares to journey to the home where this sick servant is suffering, the centurion stops him.

The centurion was brave enough to approach Jesus with his request. He was confident enough in Jesus's power that he had asked for a healing miracle in the first place. He hesitated not at all to go to the Lord. Optics or opinions of his peers are of no concern to him. But the moment Jesus offers actually to come to his home, to go to the place where he eats and sleeps and rests after a long day of soldiering, the centurion throws up a wall, "Only say the word and my servant will be healed" (Matthew 8:8)

Jesus is amazed at this man's confidence in his power. "Amen, I say to you, in no one in Israel have I found such faith" (Matthew 8:10). Here is a man, of a different background and creed, who has somehow developed an abundant faith in Jesus's power. Unafraid of criticism, and with a bold proclamation that Jesus can heal even if he isn't in the same room as the sick servant, this centurion has a faith rooted in his own amazement at Jesus's authority.

But the centurion's faith, for some reason, keeps Jesus at a distance, showing us the insecurity and fear of this high-ranking soldier. He confesses that he is not worthy to have Jesus enter his home—the place where he eats and sleeps, where he takes off his military uniform and relaxes after a long day. Jesus is mighty and powerful and can heal his servant—the centurion believes this. But even with his marvelous faith, this centurion soldier, who wields authority himself, whose name is likely known by everyone in the town and certainly by the soldiers who answer to him each day, feels as if he is unworthy to let Jesus come too close.

When we kneel during Mass in these moments just before receiving Communion, we must be completely, genuinely who we are and as we are. Whether centurions, servants, townspeople, soldiers, or busy parents, we bring to Communion our messy lives that sometimes distract us. We carry our confusion about particular Eucharistic teachings that confuse us. We acknowledge our unworthiness and ask Jesus to say "the word," the good word that will make us whole again. That is the word my little sister wanted to know all those years ago and the one that our seven-year-old confidently knew must be *Amen*.

Body of Christ, Amen. Blood of Christ, Amen.

We rise then, up off our knees, to join the Communion procession—the lines of fellow believers, fellow sinners, who are slowly, prayerfully approaching the Real Presence of Christ. We join them to partake of this saving meal, this Holy Communion. As our Eucharistic Lord is offered to us, we extend our hands or open our mouths to receive the Blessed Sacrament, despite our unworthy and messy lives, and we give ourselves over and say, "Amen!" Then we are offered the chalice, the cup of salvation, and again our Eucharistic Lord is offered to us, and we again respond, "Amen!" In doing so we are saying, "Yes, I accept that this is Christ truly present for me to receive and so to be made whole again."

Now, when my little sister asked our pastor what the word was way back in second grade, she understood *word* to mean a single word. But the scriptural evidence invites us to a more expansive understanding, to recognizing and trusting that the word of Jesus (the things he has told us) is trustworthy and so also should be our word—honest and true. When we say, "Amen!" we give assent to the holy mystery of Christ present to us in Holy Communion. That changes us, heals us, and makes us new again each and every time we receive.

Thinking and Growing as Parents

Reflect on the following questions by yourself, and then talk through your responses with your spouse, another important adult in your child's life, a good friend, or a spiritual guide.

1. What are you usually thinking about before you receive Communion? Is there any particular prayer you pray before or after you receive? Or are you maybe more often distracted by the million tasks facing you in the day and week ahead?
2. If so, how might you form a deeper habit of focusing on Mass?
3. Have you ever felt as if Jesus has said "the word" to you? Similar to a "Come and see" moment as described in chapter 1, have you had a distinct encounter with the Lord, maybe even at Mass, in a way that was particularly personal?
4. What do you think of the centurion's faith and bravery? Was that courageous or reckless both to approach Jesus unannounced and to speak to Jesus so boldly? Do you think you would have had the same confidence in Jesus to heal?
5. Is there any particular phrase or action during Mass that stumps or confuses you? What is it? How can you find responses to your questions?
6. Have you ever doubted that Christ is truly present in Holy Communion, that the Eucharistic species (the consecrated bread and wine) are the physical presence of Christ? Have you ever hesitated to say, "Amen"? If so, what was going on in your mind and heart? What are the steps you want to take to better understand the Catholic teachings on this mystery?

Growing Together as Parents and Children

Read about the healing of a centurion's servant in the Gospels of Matthew and Luke (Matthew 8:5–13 or Luke 7:1–10). Pay attention to how the centurion is so confident in what Jesus can do that he doesn't hesitate to make his request. Use the sample script to spark conversations about how we, like the centurion, proclaim our unworthiness, and our faith, at every Mass, moments before receiving the Blessed Sacrament.

Sample Script

When the centurion soldier goes to Jesus, he makes a simple request: Heal my servant. The servant is really sick and suffering a lot, and in his worry and concern, the centurion goes to Jesus for help. This is really important, though: The centurion isn't necessarily someone who would have been a follower of Jesus, not at first, and not really publicly. He was a figure of authority for the Roman Empire, meaning he likely wouldn't have been the friendliest or most attentive to Jesus and his followers. But he still asks Jesus for help. He has some faith, enough to go to Jesus with this bold request.

1. Have you ever asked Jesus for something? Why did you go to him with this prayer?
2. What do you think it felt like for the centurion to ask Jesus for help to heal his servant? Do you think he was scared Jesus couldn't do it, or would ignore him?

Jesus listens closely to the centurion's request, and he is ready to go to his home to heal the servant, but the centurion tells him to just "say the word" and the servant will be healed. The centurion knows Jesus has power. He believes Jesus can do something miraculous. And he thinks Jesus doesn't even need to come over to his house to do it!

3. How do you think the centurion became so confident in Jesus? Where might his faith have come from?

The centurion says something to Jesus that we now say a variation of at Mass, right before we go up to receive Communion. He says: "Lord, do not trouble yourself, for I am not worthy to have you enter under my roof. Therefore, I did not consider myself worthy to come to you; but say the word and let my servant be healed" (Luke 7:6–7).

This was the prayer of the centurion: for Jesus to only say the word and something miraculous would happen—a sick man would be healed.

4. Do you think you have that kind of faith, that all Jesus has to do is "say the word" and something happens? Who and what experiences have helped you have faith in the healing power of Jesus?

Shortly before we go to Communion at Mass, the priest lifts up the chalice and the host for all of us to see—although sometimes it's hard to see in crowded churches. The priest tells us to behold, or look at, the Blessed Sacrament, and he reminds us that there is Jesus, who takes away not only our sins, but the sins of *the world*. That means the whole world! What mighty power our God has to wipe away all sins, if people believe and trust, as did the centurion in the Bible story. Jesus can take away our sins, Jesus can heal us, Jesus feeds us, and we are blessed to be at this supper, this festive banquet, this holy meal.

5. What is your favorite memory of a special meal? What was the occasion? Who was there? What did you eat? And how did you feel during and after the celebration?
6. What do you think about calling Mass "The Lord's Supper," a special celebration and meal? If you could do one thing to help Mass seem closer to the memory we just talked about, what would you do?
7. How are you feeling about receiving Holy Communion for the first time? Do you feel worthy? Do you feel ready? Are you worried about anything? Are you ready for Jesus to "say the word" and heal your soul?

When we go to receive Holy Communion, we either lift up our hands or open our mouths, and the priest, deacon, or extraordinary minister will hold up the consecrated host and say, "The Body of Christ." In that moment, however quick it may be, we get to adore Our Lord. We get to gaze upon him and then consume Christ, take him into our bodies, and so be joined to him, and he to us at our most basic level. Christ Jesus becomes a part of us again and again, and we become part of his Body, the Church, again and again. All this, just by receiving Holy Communion! As we receive and eat the host and receive and drink from the chalice, we are united to Jesus and to everyone in the Church in joyful celebration.

8. After the priest, deacon, or extraordinary minister says to us, "Body of Christ," we respond, "Amen!" And then we walk to the minister serving from the chalice and hear, "Blood of Christ," and we again respond, "Amen!" What do you think the word *Amen* means? Do you say that word at any other part of your life? When?

The word comes from our most ancient ancestors in faith, our Jewish brothers and sisters. It has been translated a number of times over from Hebrew, Aramaic, Greek, Latin, and now into this English version, which basically means "So be it!" or "Yes, truly!" Basically, when we say, "Amen," we are saying yes to or agreeing with what was just said: that Christ is present in Holy Communion, and we are ready to receive him.

Sometimes you will hear people say, "Amen," when they hear something they really like. If Father says something really noteworthy in the homily, or if they hear someone declare something profound, some people will nod their heads in agreement and say, "Amen!" Sometimes people even say it when something is silly, like "This is the best cheeseburger in the whole world!" and someone else, who also really likes that cheeseburger, responds, "Amen!"

When we receive Communion, we get to say, in front of Jesus and the whole congregation in church with us, that we believe we are to receive and consume the Body and Blood of Christ. "That is Jesus! Truly! So be it! I agree!"

Praying as a Family

Wrap up your conversation in prayer. You might pray spontaneously, by saying aloud to the Lord whatever is on your heart and encouraging your child or the children with you to do the same. Or pray this simple prayer we offer here. Or, better yet, pray in both ways!

Lord,
We believe it is you in the Eucharist that we adore,
receive, consume, and praise.
It is truly you, and you want to be close to us.
Show us we are worthy to receive you.
Remind us of your deep and perfect love.
Give us faith like the centurion
and confidence that you can heal us with just one word.
Help us to say, "Amen!" with hope in your promises.
Show us your goodness and love.
Amen.

5.

Leave Different Than We Came

Joining Our Stories to the Church's Story

Tommy: After-Mass Donuts

"6:30? Really? They come that early?" I was stumped. Katie was going on excitedly about a new event she'd started for her youth group, but I couldn't believe that teenagers were willingly going to a 6:30 a.m. Mass on a weekday during summer vacation.

"Free coffee and donuts after, so yeah, they show up!" my long-distance girlfriend—soon-to-be fiancée—happily explained. "Msgr. Gaddy said I could pay for the coffee and donuts at CC's with the youth-ministry credit card, so the promise of it being free really helps. And, you know, first they get to go to Mass!" She was so excited, so I just let her gush for a little bit before agreeing to come when I finally moved down to Louisiana in three weeks.

"I'll give the talk and lesson, if that helps," I offered.

"Oh, no talk. No lesson. It isn't Bible study after Mass. It's just Mass and then hanging out at a coffee shop after. Just Jesus and java," Katie quickly informed me.

Stumped again, I asked, "No youth-group talk?"

"Nope. Just go to Mass and then spend some time together," she explained.

"That's it?"

"Yes, that's it! And it's enough!" Katie snapped.

"Sorry, sorry. I'm not criticizing. I guess I just didn't think teenagers would do a youth-group thing without youth-group things part of it," I tried to explain, not fully capturing my confusion.

"We just want to get them to Mass. The point is Mass, and the free coffee and donuts get them there. Mass is the youth-group thing. Everything else would just be extra," Katie said, a little more calmly, even though she had every right to be annoyed with me. "You'll see when you get down here. It's really cool."

Sure enough, three weeks later, as a brand-new resident of Lake Charles, Louisiana, I woke up in my freshly set-up apartment and made my way to Our Lady, Queen of Heaven for the 6:30 morning Mass. *This is for my girlfriend, soon-to-be fiancée, for my girlfriend, soon-to-be fiancée*, I thought to myself. Back then, I was far from a morning person—though marriage and children have turned me into a 4:30 a.m. wake-up guy—and I still couldn't square the circle that teenagers would get up so early during their precious no-school days to go to Mass, just because of free coffee and donuts.

But as I walked into the church, where Katie and I would later get married, there were about thirty-five teenagers. A few sat together, while most sat on their own. These youngest daily Mass attendees by at least thirty to forty years spread themselves throughout the Church. Katie was standing in the back, by the sacristy stairs, whispering quietly to Msgr. Gaddy, clearly giving him an update about her newly created summer success, Jesus and Java. She was talking with both hands waving around, as is her way, and gesturing to the kids in the pews. As I walked up, Monsignor had a huge smile on his face, pulled her into a side hug, and said, "Whatever gets them here! Jesus, java, a text-message invite. Proud of you, kid! Let's give them heaven!" And then, clicking his lapel microphone on, Monsignor said, "Please rise," and Mass began.

Forty-five minutes later, dozens of cars pulled into the parking lot of CC's Coffee House, a cute little coffee-and-donut shop just three turns away from the parish. We poured in, the teens all knowing the drill: Line up, step forward, and place your coffee order, keeping it to under five dollars. Then Katie would order four dozen donuts, of varying flavors, and set the boxes out on the tables the group would push together. Everyone would have their drinks—from drip coffee to fancy mocha-sippies with too much whipped cream—share the donuts, visit and laugh, tell stories and take selfies. Then by 8:30 at the latest, they'd all disperse, heading back to their teenage summer days working a job, attending camps, or just lying around the house.

Katie was right. The entire model was sort of genius. Convince teenagers to start their day with Jesus, give them some java and sugary deep-fried dough as a bit of incentive, hang out with them in an entirely casual and safe setting, and let the conversation unfold.

No one walked into the coffee shop waving Bibles around, shouting, "Repent! The Gospel is at hand!" No one was preaching to the baristas, though in Louisiana, most were likely already Catholic. No one was pulling out a rosary or chanting Latin or showing off anything distinctively (or weirdly) Catholic. It was just a group of people—ranging from thirteen to forty, teenagers and young adults and a few youth-ministry volunteers—going to Mass, receiving the Eucharist, and then hanging out with one another afterward, sharing coffee and donuts and a few laughs.

We were sent forth at each Mass to go glorify the Lord with our lives, and then we would do that while sharing food and consuming caffeine. We'd go announce the Gospel of the Lord, not with loud pronouncements in the coffee shop, converting anyone we saw, but instead by speaking kindly, responding patiently, showing charity and compassion to one another and anyone else we encountered. We glorified the Lord by living life to the full, enjoying good coffee and delightful conversations together. Over the course of that summer, the group grew, seemingly week to week. And the youth and young adults grew to more deeply appreciate what Mass results in: joyful fellowship with the Lord and with one another.

Anna asked Sarah to be her Confirmation sponsor that summer. Sam started dating Becca. Michael, home from his first year of seminary, was bursting with excitement to talk about his formation for the priesthood. Jane told us she was discerning with a religious community. One Tuesday, the teens pooled their money and bought breakfast sandwiches and a few dozen donuts and brought them over to the local Catholic Charities food-distribution site.

Those early morning Masses led to fellowship and friendships. Mass drew everyone together. A growing love of the Eucharist, with a desire to receive the Eucharist together, even at the seemingly inhumane hour of 6:30 a.m. on summer Tuesdays and Fridays, was the unifying force behind teenagers waking up early for weeks to come to Church and then hang out for a little while.

At the last Jesus and Java of the summer, the Tuesday before school would begin that Wednesday, eighty-three teenagers and young adults took over the Ryan Street CC's. Katie even convinced Msgr. Gaddy to join us after Mass despite his having always been insistent that teens didn't want to hang out with an old priest. As he walked into the coffee shop, I could see tears in his eyes. While Katie was chatting with the barista and went to pay, Monsignor walked over to the counter.

"Let me." Monsignor reached into his pocket to pull out his wallet.

"I've got the parish credit card, Monsignor. Don't worry," Katie assured him.

"No, no, this one's on me. *I'm* paying, not the parish. You did it, my girl!" Monsignor pulled out some crisp hundreds and laid them on the counter as he patted her shoulder. Katie looked up at him, shrugged, and smiled, reaching out to squeeze his arm.

Msgr. Gaddy had hired Katie as his youth minister when she moved back to Lake Charles from a brief stint in Chicago. He'd given her one task: Bring the youth back to our parish. She took that job and served that parish, because he asked her to, and now, with a coffee shop full of teenagers fresh out of morning Mass, Msgr. Gaddy was paying for the coffee and donuts for the young people she'd brought back to the parish. And she'd done it not with a glitzy program or with a well-crafted talk, but just by inviting teenagers to Mass and giving them time to hang out together after.

The youth had come to Mass, first and foremost, and were now living the very mandate of the Mass as they were sent forth to proclaim the Gospel with their lives. The youth and young adults at that summer of Jesus and Java lived life to the full, glorifying the Lord, announcing the Gospel. They went forth from Mass—whether to a coffee shop a couple of times a week that summer, or to all the normal situations of life that unfold day after day—strengthened by the Eucharist and their newly discovered community. In so many wonderful ways, those young people, and we adults who tagged along with them that summer, discovered who they were as members of the Body of Christ.

Katie: "See You Friday"

The genius of Jesus and Java, a random idea I had while traveling through the Atlanta airport one weekend, was that it required very little planning. Mass is Mass. It's largely the same each time, just a variation on the readings and homily. The teens would show up (or they wouldn't), and the coffee shop would be there no matter what. The lift on my end was minimal, and as a youth minister traveling throughout the summer to speak at youth conferences and camps, I needed minimal.

My hope was to have a dozen teens in attendance. Twelve was a good-enough number for Jesus, and it would be good enough for the Teens Undivided Youth Group, the youth-ministry program at OLQH. It would probably delight every old church lady when they realized young people were at morning Mass. Realistically, I thought we'd maybe get five or six folks, and two of them would be seminarians assigned to the parish for the summer.

One Sunday afternoon's post on our youth-group Instagram page, with a hastily thrown-together caption inviting young people to "come to Mass, and get coffee and donuts on us after," led to twenty-four teens the first Tuesday we held Jesus and Java. Those numbers steadily grew throughout the summer, and on the last morning before the first day of school, we filled the coffee shop beyond capacity. Monsignor treated us all, and as we said farewell to the last teen later that morning, Tommy and I sat in a booth marveling at the success of the simplest youth-ministry event I'd ever planned or hosted.

As we sat there, chuckling at the absurd simplicity of combining Mass and donuts to attract any Catholic to come to church, the manager of CC's walked over to our table. I knew him, mostly because I had given him a heads-up in the second week of Jesus and Java that we'd be there twice a week, and I had asked if it was okay if we commandeered a section of tables. He'd been more than happy to let us, and on more than one occasion he had given me a steep discount on the dozens of donuts I was buying. "Y'all done for the summer, Katie?" he asked me, wiping the table as he gestured for one of the baristas to come over and refill our drip coffees.

"School starts tomorrow, so I think so. I have to be in my classroom by 7:15 every morning, so I can make morning Mass at 6:30 on Tuesdays and Fridays, but probably can't come here after. The teens might come by, though. Their bell doesn't ring until 7:40, so they'd have time. It just won't be me paying for it anymore!"

"I sure hope so. They bring a lotta life into this place," he mused, wiping down another table.

"They really do, don't they?"

"Polite and kind. Always said thank you. Good Catholic kids, that group."

"I'm proud of them," I remarked, thinking of how over the course of just a few weeks, these young people had made early morning Mass and fellowship and friendship a priority within their summer. Most of them came every week, and many of them invited friends. They maybe first showed up because of the free food, but they kept coming back because of the chance to worship together and then sit and spend time with one another. The ridiculous simplicity—break bread at the altar and then break bread at the coffee shop—astounded and pleased me to no end.

Tommy and I got up to leave, anxious to get some last-minute errands in on our last day of summer before the school year began the next day.

"Thanks again, Katie," the manager said. "I'll see you Friday."

"Oh, well, I'll be at Mass, but can't get here. Drop-off line duty, and all," I quickly remarked.

"I know," he said. "I'll see you at Mass. The teens invited me to join them."

Learning from Scripture

Blessed, Broken, Given

Mass isn't just for us. We go to sit at the Lord's feet, listen to his Word, rejoice in his presence, and receive him in Holy Communion for our own sanctification, but also for the sake of the whole world. Mass is where we receive all this goodness, given freely. Mass is where we go to receive all the Lord has for us. But we don't keep that goodness all to ourselves. We are, in fact, sent out at the end of Mass to go and proclaim, announce, and give witness to what has happened to us and for us at Mass. What we have received and consumed—the Body and Blood of Christ—is who we are now to be in the world. We are told to *go* at the end of Mass to be the presence of Christ in our homes and neighborhoods, cities and towns. We are to be the face, the hands and feet, and the faithful presence of Christ in our world.

Sometimes this means just being the polite group at the coffee shop. Other times, it means being the polite group of teens that invites the manager of that coffee shop to start coming to daily Mass too. Either way, we leave the Mass different than we came. Having heard the Word and consumed the Eucharist, we are sent forth on a mission. The Mass has ended, but we are changed forever. And now, driven by that change, we step out to change the world.

No one learned this better—that an encounter with the Lord changes you forever—than the two disciples who met Jesus on the road to Emmaus following the Resurrection Sunday. If you aren't familiar with the whole story, read the Gospel of Luke 24:13–35.

Leaving Jerusalem after the turmoil of the Passover and Jesus's Crucifixion, they are headed out of town to step away from the noise and mess and simply process all that has occurred. On the road, they encounter Jesus who, as if in some sort of resurrected incognito mode, is totally unrecognizable to them. As they walk and talk, Cleopas and his companion are almost stunned that this stranger doesn't seem to know about the dramatic events of the previous days. But they share the story, they eventually listen to what Jesus (whom they don't yet know is Jesus) has to say, and when they finally arrive at their destination for the night, they invite this stranger to stay for dinner.

Whatever he said, and however he explained all that occurred, it moves these disciples so deeply that they insist Jesus remain with them a little while longer. And Jesus does stay with them, at least for a little while. They sit at the table, and as Jesus takes the bread, blesses it, breaks it, and gives it to them, they immediately see who he is. This is Jesus, the man who blessed, broke, and distributed bread to more than five thousand people on a hillside near Bethsaida. Here is the one who blessed, broke, and distributed bread at the Last Supper in Jerusalem. This is the one they thought was dead, but is now, quite clearly, alive. Again he is blessing, breaking, and giving them bread. The moment they recognize him, he vanishes.

But it isn't that Jesus has been magicked away with some elaborate illusion. When they recognize him as he is breaking, blessing, and distributing bread, they realize he is fully present to them, in that moment, within that meal, with particular words and actions. Jesus is there, in their midst, and without hesitation they realize their very hearts were burning within them from the moment they'd first encountered him along the road.

The story about the disciples on the road to Emmaus has similarities with going to Mass. The disciples break open the Word, share a meal with the Lord, receive what is freely given, and upon realizing they've been changed by the entire encounter, they rush out to go and tell everyone else about it. "They set out at once," it says in Luke 24:33, with no hesitation. They've been so deeply moved that they can't keep their joy to themselves, so they return to Jerusalem and find Jesus's apostles and proclaim this essential truth that has rooted the Church for centuries and is our foundation to this very day: "He was made known to them in the breaking of the bread" (Luke 24:35).

Go...

When we go to Mass, we bring all of ourselves—messes, mistakes, wounds, and weariness. All of who we are ought to come and sit at the feet of Jesus, listening to his Word, rejoicing at his presence there and in Holy Communion. Mass is meant to transform us, both inside and out. There's no way it couldn't, if we are able to open ourselves up to that transformation. We are different as a result of going to Mass and receiving the Eucharist, and Mass ends not with a pat on the back and a congratulations for attending, but with a command to *go out and tell others* about what has just happened.

When Cleopas and his companion encounter Jesus on the road to Emmaus, they unpack the scriptures and then share a meal. Their hearts burn throughout this encounter, and they're compelled to rush back to Jerusalem to share their story. They meet Jesus, share food with Jesus, and are changed by Jesus. Their joy becomes so great that they have to go and tell everyone else about Jesus. Today, thousands of years later, we get to do the same thing. Each of us, in our unique circumstances in life, is on a road to Emmaus. We are journeying, walking along the road of life, making decisions and having conversations and managing the myriad responsibilities that come our way. But at every Mass, when Jesus comes alongside us and begins to walk with us for a stretch of the road, we unpack the scriptures, share a meal, and give ourselves to Christ; and he gives himself wholly and completely to us. Such a profound encounter ought to leave our hearts burning, compelling us to go tell everyone else about Jesus.

Often, however, we get to the end of Mass distracted, ready to go, grabbing bags and jackets and turning phone notifications back on. Half the time, we miss the concluding words, and we just quickly murmur our response of gratitude while begging a tiny child to stop hanging off the end of the pew. Still, we say *thanks*—to God, giver of all good gifts. Pay attention next time it is the end of Mass. Check your attention to the sending forth, the charge to *go*, that we all receive.

It can perhaps feel a little daunting to hear a charge to go and do *more* things in our already quite busy and somewhat complicated lives. The Church wants me to go do more than I'm already doing? Where exactly? And how? Between work and home and family responsibilities and the many things that pile up day after day, it may seem that leaving Mass shouldn't include another chore.

But we can't think of these final moments of Mass as a command to just go do some work for which we have no time, or are ill-equipped or unprepared. We have just been in the presence of the Lord, sung his glory, received his Word. We have eaten true food and true drink and been fortified by the grace of receiving Holy Communion. Now we are sent out, recognizing that the hearts burning within us are entirely prepared to do precisely this work of building up the kingdom of God. We are the most prepared, the most equipped, and hopefully the most joyful we can be. And it is precisely the right time. How will you go forth?

Thinking and Growing as Parents

Reflect on the following questions by yourself, and then talk through your responses with your spouse, another important adult in your child's life, a good friend, or a spiritual guide. Or maybe you prefer to journal or sit in church or another quiet space and reflect on these things.

1. How do you feel when you leave Mass? Are you at peace? Stressed about what's coming next in the day? Excited to go talk about what you've experienced?
2. Has anyone ever shared with you about what Mass has meant to them or how it has impacted them? What did they say? How did that change you?

3. Have you ever had the chance to tell someone about how the Eucharist has changed your life?
4. How do you think the disciples on the road to Emmaus felt when they realized it was Jesus in the breaking of the bread? How do you think you would have felt?
5. What do you think it means to announce the Gospel with your life? How can you glorify the Lord in your daily life?

Growing Together as Parents and Children

Read the story about the road to Emmaus in the Gospel of Luke, chapter 24, verses 13–35. Notice how the disciples who are walking to Emmaus are surprised by Jesus, but are then really comforted by his presence, even when they don't yet know who he is. Use the sample script to spark conversation and discussion about how we encounter Jesus in the Mass and recognize him in the breaking of the bread.

Sample Script

Let's talk a little about this gospel story about Jesus and two disciples on the road to a place called Emmaus.

1. Have you ever gone on a long trip? What did you do on the way there? What was it like to be on that journey?
2. The disciples on the road to Emmaus are joined by Jesus on their journey (but they don't yet know it's him). How do you think the disciples felt having a stranger start walking and talking to them? Do you think they were excited, or nervous? How would you feel?
3. What do you think they learned as they walked with Jesus?

Emmaus is about seven miles away from Jerusalem. In Jesus's time, the disciples walking there would probably have given themselves the whole day to get there, walking at a fairly casual pace. They're chatting about everything that's happened, so let's recall what happened: Jesus triumphantly entered Jerusalem, which we remember on Palm Sunday each year, and then he shared with his disciples a final Passover meal. Passover is a very important meal prepared and eaten by Jewish people (as Jesus was) in the time of Jesus and still today.

After the meal, Jesus went to the Garden of Gethsemane to pray. There he was arrested and taken to Pontius Pilate, who had him whipped, beaten, and a crown of thorns placed on Jesus's head. After all of that, Pilate condemned Jesus to death. Jesus was forced to carry his cross, was crucified, died, and then was buried.

But Jesus was raised from the dead on the third day. As the disciples in our gospel story are walking along, thinking and talking about all of this, Jesus starts walking with them, and they tell Jesus that their Lord's body wasn't in the tomb, but they don't know what it means.

Jesus then explains everything, talking about Moses and the prophets, explaining all the signs and wonders and symbols. He helps them process everything that has happened, and then they invite him to stay for dinner. They don't know it's Jesus. But they know that they like being with him and listening to him.

4. How do you think you would feel if Jesus was walking with you and explaining everything directly to you? Would that comfort you? Would that help you? Do you think you'd know it was Jesus?

When Jesus blesses and breaks the bread, then distributes it among everyone, the disciples suddenly realize who he is. It is when he shares a meal with them, doing what he did at the Last Supper, that they instantly recognize him. They see that it is Jesus. When he gives them the Eucharist, they see that it is him. Centuries ago, on a dirt road walking to a faraway town, Jesus broke open the scriptures, and then at a dinner table in Emmaus, he broke the bread. He is made known to them, their hearts burn within them, and they are changed forever.

When we go to Mass now, Jesus is made known to us in the breaking of the bread. It's like we are walking to Emmaus when we pray the Mass. We, too, are unpacking the scriptures and we are listening to the Word. We are sharing a meal and encountering Jesus in the breaking of, and receiving of, his Body and Blood.

And that absolutely changes us. This isn't some ordinary thing or some boring meal. This is an encounter with Christ Jesus, and we can't keep that to ourselves, can we? If you have really good news, what do you do with it? You want to share it! These disciples who meet Jesus, share a meal with him, and come to see that it is him—they get up and rush back to Jerusalem to tell everyone else that they saw, met, and spent time with Jesus! They shout it from the rooftops. They announce it joyfully! They just can't keep it to themselves!

When Mass ends, after we have done all the things we do in Mass, the priest says a final prayer, gives us a final blessing, then tells us to *go*! Go forth, go announce, go glorify, go in peace! Leave Mass, and go on another journey.

In the gospel story of Cleopas and his companion meeting Jesus on the road to Emmaus, these two disciples went back to Jerusalem to tell the other followers of Jesus that they had met Jesus, risen from the dead.

5. Who will you go tell about meeting our risen Lord in the Eucharist? Whom can you share the beauty of Communion with?
6. Who has shared this Eucharistic joy with you? Who has helped you learn more about the Mass and helped you prepare for your First Communion? Who have been your companions on this journey?
7. Is there something you would like to tell important people in your faith journey? Anything you would like to do for them? Let's write their names down and think about how you can share your joy and gratitude with them.

If time allows now, fill out this list of names with ideas of ways your child can share the joy of his or her faith journey with them. For example, perhaps your child can write thank-you notes, draw pictures, or make phone calls to godparents, grandparents, teachers, classmates, or others who have played an important role in helping him or her get ready for First Communion.

Praying as a Family

Wrap up your conversation in prayer. You might pray spontaneously, by saying aloud to the Lord whatever is on your heart and encouraging your child or the children with you to do the same. Or pray this simple prayer we offer here. Or, better yet, pray in both ways!

Jesus,
You are made known to us in the breaking of the bread.
Give us eyes to see you walking beside us on the journey
of our lives.
Help us understand that you are with us always,
that we receive you into our bodies in Holy Communion,
and that you give us strength to leave each Mass

ready to share our joy in knowing you with the world.
Thank you for drawing close to us and letting us be close
to you.
And so, we joyfully say, Amen!

Epilogue

Same Jesus in Rome or Lake Charles!

Katie: He Let Me Receive Him

One morning, on the way to school, just after we had passed by Our Lady Queen of Heaven and waved "hi" to Jesus, Rose piped up from the back seat. "Mom, when's my First Communion again?"

"May 10, bud. Daddy's birthday."

"Is that before or after Blessed Carlo becomes Saint Carlo?"

I should share that our family has a significant devotion to Blessed Carlo Acutis—who was made a saint on September 7, 2025—for a variety of reasons. My husband kind of looks like him. Though he is not Italian and Carlo wasn't Irish, there's something about dark, curly headed, not particularly tall men that puts them all in the same club. I had grown to love Carlo when I learned of his love of technology and how he studied coding and web design so he could share the beauty of Eucharistic miracles online. Carlo wanted to share the faith in the spaces and places people were, even digitally, and as someone working in and around the world of social and traditional media, I claimed Carlo as a patron. And Rose, all seven years of her at the time, loved Carlo because he was a kid, not unlike her. He loved playing outside, soccer, and Pokémon. He liked to go hiking with his family and was kind to his friends. The only thing Rose wanted for Christmas that year was a relic of Blessed Carlo, to keep with her at school, so her heavenly best buddy would always be with her. Clare, our precocious four-year-old, loved Carlo because of a single photo she saw of him one time holding a cat. She was sold. Best future saint ever. Because of our love of Carlo, a family patron, we made plans to go to his canonization in Rome, which had been scheduled for April 27, 2025.

"After his canonization, bud," I told Rose. "April 27 is before May 10. So we'll go to Rome, get home April 29, and then your First Communion will be about two weeks later."

"Oh. Okay." Rose suddenly got very quiet.

"Everything okay?" I quickly asked, worried something was suddenly wrong.

"No, it's fine."

I knew she wasn't fine. "Are you sure, bud? It's okay. Say what you want to say."

Rose sighed, and then in one quick breath, she said, "I just thought it might be nice to receive the Eucharist at his canonization Mass in Rome, with the pope, so that I can receive Jesus the same day we celebrate Carlo being with Jesus in heaven."

"Slow down there, kiddo. You want to receive First Communion at Carlo's canonization?"

"Could I?" she asked, with zero hesitation.

I wondered aloud, "Uh . . . maybe?"

Every Catholic connection I'd fostered over the years, from folks at the Vatican to my sister the nun, began bouncing around my mind. Who do I call to make that happen? Do I have to ask permission? Could she receive from the pope? So I promised Rose I'd look into it, and after a few phone calls, a chat with our dear friend Fr. Patrick Mary Briscoe, who was coming to Rome with us, and a conversation between Tommy, our pastor, and me, we decided it'd be best for Rose to make her First Communion a few days before Carlo's canonization in Rome. Then, she'd be able to receive at the canonization itself, for which we had good seats because of those connections that have so graced my life and my family's life.

The day before we were to leave for Rome—plans in place, bags packed, including the First Communion dress, with Rose ready and eager—we woke to the news that Pope Francis had died. Because of my job as a CNN Vatican Analyst and my work on SiriusXM's The Catholic Channel, I couldn't travel to Rome, because I needed work stateside. We had to postpone our pilgrimage to Rome.

Of all the sad and hard moments in those immediate days following Pope Francis's death, the hardest thing of all was sitting Rose down and telling her we weren't going to Rome for the canonization of Blessed Carlo. Rose was understandably upset (we all were), but then, with a joy and optimism that only a seven-year-old can have in a moment such as that, she asked me, "Mom, I still get to make First Communion at some point, right?"

"Well of course, bud. You'll do it on May 10 as first planned, with your classmates. At St. Margaret's."

"Then that'll be great, too, mom. Same Jesus in Rome or Lake Charles! I get to receive either way!" *Same Jesus in Rome or Lake Charles* . . . out of the mouth of a little girl who had just been deeply disappointed, but who now had hope in the promise of the Eucharist, whether in Rome, the heart of Catholic Church, or at our home parish.

On May 10, 2025, just two days after the world was introduced to Pope Leo XIV for the first time, Rose received her First Communion. Our family heard "Leo, our pope" for the first time in the Eucharistic Prayer at that Mass where thirty-one second-graders received Jesus, the same Jesus as in Rome and in every tabernacle throughout the world, for the first time.

When the First Communion Mass was over, and we met Rose in the school cafeteria at the parish's reception, she came running up to us. "Mom! Dad! That was really Jesus! And he let *me* receive him!"

"Yeah, bud. Pretty amazing, even in Lake Charles!"

"Oh, Mom, the *best* in Lake Charles. We have to tell everyone we know they have to come get some Jesus!" True to form, for weeks after, any chance Rose got, she'd tell everyone—including my Catholic connections and colleagues at a number of speaking events I brought her to—that she'd made her First Communion and they should receive Jesus too.

Tommy: Come Get Jesus

Katie is always quick to include me and the girls in her travels. If she can find a way to bring us along to a speaking or radio event, she does, which means the girls and I have visited the top of the iconic stadium at the University of Notre Dame, seen green rooms and backstage speaker areas, walked across stages in dozens of arenas and event centers, spent time at a lot of parishes and chanceries, and seen the beauty and power of youth conferences and adult gatherings of Catholics all across the United States.

A month after Rose's First Communion, we traveled with Katie to Franciscan University of Steubenville for the first youth conference on campus. Katie was hosting, working, while the girls and I hung out and swam at the hotel pool. Of all the very cool places we have taken our girls, including the tippy top of the Notre Dame stadium, our girls are somehow enamored most with the indoor pool at the Best Western Hotel in Steubenville, Ohio.

We swam for hours each day, and by Saturday night of the conference, with shriveled fingers and exhausted legs, I hoisted myself out of the pool to sit on the side while Rose and Clare played around in the shallow end. A burly gentleman I didn't know walked in and cannonballed into the deep end—much to the girls' delight—and a few minutes later, he and I got to chatting.

He was a charter-bus driver, having driven a group to the conference from near Philadelphia. I went to college in Philadelphia, at Eastern University, and as I shared that tidbit, he lit up, explaining that he was the bus driver the previous semester for the women's softball team at Eastern. They seemed to have loved the man and had given him team merch.

Pleasantries and chitchat unfolded, and when the girls got tired and needed dinner, we said our goodbyes to the bus driver, who continued to lounge in the pool. Nice guy, nice conversation, and I didn't think of it again until the next morning at breakfast in the hotel lobby. There was the bus driver sitting at a high-top table alone, wearing his Eastern University women's softball T-shirt. I said good morning to him, helped situate the girls with their pancakes and yogurt, and just as I was going to get coffees, he struck up another conversation with me.

He was chatty, asking me all sorts of questions about the type of school Eastern is, what I thought of the particular university across the street where the conference was, and what the gathering was all about. He was curious and seemed not to have talked much to anyone for a couple of days. He'd driven the bus of teens, got his room at the hotel, watched TV, swam at the pool, ordered some food, and now seemed eager for interaction.

When he got up to go a few minutes later, I waved goodbye to him, and he wandered over to our table and struck up our conversation again. But this time, rather than ask me about the conference, he shared what all the teens had been talking about on the seven-hour bus ride from Philly over to Steubenville.

"They were so excited, I tell ya. Just so excited. Talking about the music and the talks and this adoration thing. I don't really remember what that is. I went to Catholic school. In fact, I've got a bunch of Catholic jokes—I told some of them on the bus, and they laughed." He proceeded to tell us a joke, and we politely laughed. And then, just as we thought he was about to walk away, he said something that instantly caught Katie's attention.

"Ya know, if I'd had something like this when I was a kid, there's no telling where my faith would be," he mused. He got quiet, thoughtful, and just as he was about to walk away, Katie piped up.

"Well, why don't you walk over and join us for Mass this morning? It starts around 10:30, I think. We'd love to have you."

"Mass, huh?" the man responded, a little taken aback by the quick invitation.

"Mass! Where we get Jesus! Come with us!" Rose gleefully shouted. And then she began talking all about her First Communion, telling this nice bus driver, whose name we didn't even know, the details of our canceled Rome trip and how Mass is the best thing ever and he should totally join us, no questions asked. The bus driver blinked in stunned silence, nodding politely as Rose gushed forth more than he probably wanted to know.

Katie reiterated the invitation. "You'd absolutely be welcome to join us for Mass. I'm hosting the conference, so just tell them I invited you if you decide to come." The man nodded his thanks and left the breakfast area. Katie finished eating, then rushed off to campus and the conference. The girls and I packed up our rooms, loaded the minivan, and drove over to campus by 10:00 so we could grab a seat before Mass. I think all four of us completely forgot about the bus driver—until 10:15 sharp.

The girls and I were seated, waiting for Mass to begin, and watching the conference-goers gathering, when the bus driver strolled over, escorted by two of the conference staff. He was dressed in a three-piece suit, wearing a wool fedora, and as Clare quickly pointed out, carrying a cane with an eagle's head handle. He pointed to Katie, still up on the stage, and said, "Her. That's her. That's the woman who invited me to Mass." I quickly ducked over to the conference staff to confirm that, yes, we had indeed invited the bus driver to Mass. A few minutes later I saw the program director chat with Katie when she got off stage. After the surprise left her face, she smiled broadly and looked over to where the bus driver was now sitting next to me and the girls. She was absolutely delighted, and maybe a little stunned, to see him there.

Our new friend took up three chairs, and he kept a giant smile across his face the entire Mass. He leaned over at one point and whispered—maybe not as quietly as he intended—that this was absolutely the most beautiful thing he'd ever seen. And, after Mass had ended, he gave us hugs, thanked us profusely for inviting him, and said, "This saved me."

Katie and I just sat there chuckling to ourselves, absolutely gobsmacked that a random invite to a random guy that we'd mostly forgotten about had resulted in his returning to Mass. But Rose wasn't surprised. In fact, she stood there beaming and said very matter-of-factly, "Well, of course he came. We told him to come get Jesus. Who turns down a chance to do that?"

Who turns down that chance, indeed! And getting little ones excited about that, helping them to understand what is happening, and why, and building excitement in their little hearts for the great privilege and grace it is to receive the Eucharist, is the highest honor and the greatest challenge we will ever face.

First Communion preparation is not just about teaching little ones what to say when, or how to sit, stand, or kneel properly during Mass. It isn't just about learning the responses or memorizing a set of prayers. Preparing a little one for the first time they will receive Communion is preparing a child to "get Jesus" in a new way. We help a child meet Jesus and choose to come and see all he has to offer. We get to help a child sit at Christ's feet and listen attentively to all he has to say to their anxious and worried hearts. We spend time forming a child to see that Jesus feeds them, not with mere food and drink, but with his very self. We help them contemplate this remarkable mystery of God present with us, which lies at the center of our Catholic faith. And we get to teach a child to be sent, to go forth at the end of Mass and be the presence of Christ in their world—loving, inviting, caring for those in need all around them, and letting them know that Jesus came to save them and remains even now with us.

That's what we get to do when we prepare children for First Communion. And doing so hopefully stirs within us, too, a deeper understanding and love of the Eucharist. This will be a lifelong journey. Just as we grow in all other areas of our lives, our faith journey should help us grow in understanding and in relationship with Jesus. We adults also should come and see and be changed by the Eucharist.

We're praying for you as you undertake this work and welcome the gift of joy it can bring. We are lifting you up at all the Masses we go to, even the ones where we get distracted by our squirmy kids. This is a great honor, and we know you can do it. We hope this little book of ours has helped you do just that.

Acknowledgments

We can't write these books—or anything, for that matter—without the incredible guidance of the amazing team at Ave Maria Press. There is no one better in this business, no other publisher that brings the most unique and insightful works to print. All that Ave has given us over the years, especially in friendship, has made our lives infinitely better. And to our singularly talented editor, Eileen Ponder: These books exist because of your insights and wisdom. Thank you, Eileen.

To our family, especially our parents and Sister Lilianna Petra, our Wawa, who prayed for us particularly often during this book's journey to the page—thanks for loving us and helping us so we can write.

And to our extended Sisters of Life family, who have kept us in prayer every day for the past two years, if not longer. Never did we imagine we'd have more than 120 sister-aunties for our girls, but here we are! Thank you for being the joyful gift that each of you is.

To our friends, especially the ones we've hung out with in person over the past year, who have shared meals with us, entertained our children, listened to our woes, supported our dreams, and prayed for us. What a gift to be able to look at you all and say, "Ah, you too? I thought it was just us!" Thank you for your companionship on the journey.

To our Hallow family, who have given us so much room to be creative with *Family Mass Prep* and so many other projects to help families pray—thank you for giving us space and support to create beautiful things for the Lord.

To Katie's colleagues at SiriusXM and Tommy's coworkers at LCCP, NFCYM, and iteach—working alongside you all is a joy and honor, and we love that we get to stand at the water cooler and share life with you.

To the many priests who know, love, and serve our family. When you pray for us, say Mass for us, come eat with us, and answer our texts and calls, know that your steadfast presence in our lives is a remarkable gift to each and every one of us. You're good spiritual dads, and you know who you are. There are too many of you to list, but we have your numbers, and you'll get a text.

Lastly, to our girls, Rose and Clare. You help us love Jesus more and more each day, and we hope we're doing the same for you. Thanks for being your wiggly, wonderful selves, even—and especially—at Mass. Saying hi to Jesus with you two, and receiving Christ as a family, is the best and most beautiful thing we could ever hope to do. Although, we do hope that one day you will appreciate that trip to the top of Notre Dame stadium!

Appendix

Prayers for Children and Parents

Prayers for Children

Adapted from prayers attributed to St. Thomas Aquinas

Prayer Before Mass

Dear Jesus,
I am here to see you.
I want to receive the Eucharist so I can be close to you,
even though sometimes it feels like I'm far away.
I want to stand in your light, and receive all that you have to give me.

Heal me. Cleanse me. Wash me of my sins.
Help me see your goodness.
Help me receive your gifts.
Help me stand in your presence.

I want to receive this bread of angels, the King of Kings and Lord of Lords,
With humility, purity, and faith.
Show me that receiving you will bring me to salvation.
Remind me of the reality of your presence in the Blessed Sacrament.

As I receive your Body, born from the Virgin Mary,
help me to be received into your mystical Body
and counted as one of your own.

Loving Father,
As I receive your beloved son, in this sacrament,
Help me to one day see him face to face in glory.
I love you, Lord. I am here to see and receive you.
Amen.

A Child's Thanksgiving After Mass

Father, all powerful, thank you.
Thank you for bringing me close to the precious Body & Blood of your son,
Our Lord Jesus Christ.
I have made mistakes.
I have been far from you.
But you have given me the Eucharist, and I am grateful to receive it.

May this Eucharist be a shield and guard me.
May this Eucharist purify and protect me.
May this Eucharist help me grow in faith, humility, patience, obedience, and love.
May this Eucharist strengthen me, unite me to you, and lead me safely through this life each day.

Please continue to lead me, even when I stumble and fall,
to be close to you, so that one day I will be a saint with you in heaven.
Amen.

Prayers for Parents

Prayers attributed to St. Thomas Aquinas

A Prayer Before Mass

Almighty and ever-living God,
I approach the sacrament
of your only-begotten son
our Lord Jesus Christ,
I come sick to the doctor of life,
unclean to the fountain of mercy,

blind to the radiance of eternal light,
and poor and needy to the Lord
of heaven and earth.

Lord, in your great generosity,
heal my sickness,
wash away my defilement,
enlighten my blindness, enrich my poverty,
and clothe my nakedness.
May I receive the bread of angels,
the King of Kings and Lord of Lords,
with humble reverence,
with the purity and faith,
the repentance and love,
and the determined purpose
that will help to bring me to salvation.
May I receive the sacrament
of the Lord's Body and Blood,
and its reality and power.

Kind God,
may I receive the Body
of your only-begotten son,
our Lord Jesus Christ,
born from the womb of the Virgin Mary,
and so be received into his mystical body
and numbered among his members.

Loving Father,
As on my earthly pilgrimage
I now receive your beloved son
under the veil of a sacrament,
may I one day see him face to face in glory,
who lives and reigns with you forever.
Amen.

Prayer of Thanksgiving

Lord, Father all-powerful and ever-living God,
I thank you, for even though I am a sinner,
Your unprofitable servant, not because of my worth
But in the kindness of your mercy,
You have fed me with the Precious Body and Blood
Of your Son, our Lord, Jesus Christ.
I pray that this Holy Communion may not bring me
condemnation and punishment but forgiveness and salvation.
May it be a helmet of faith and a shield of good will.
May it purify me from evil ways and put an end to my evil passions.
May it bring me charity and patience, humility and obedience, and growth in the power to do good.
May it be my strong defense against all my enemies, visible and invisible, and the perfect calming
of all my evil impulses, bodily and spiritual.
May it unite me more closely to you, the One true God, and lead me
safely through death to everlasting happiness with You.
And I pray that you will lead me, a sinner, to the banquet where you,
with the Son and Holy Spirit,
are true and perfect light, total fulfillment,
everlasting joy, gladness without end, and perfect
happiness to your saints.
Grant this through Christ our Lord.
Amen.

Katie Prejean McGrady is host of the *Ave Explores* podcast and *The Katie McGrady Show* on Sirius XM's The Catholic Channel. She is an international speaker, the author of *Room 24: Adventures of a New Evangelist* and *Follow: Your Lifelong Adventure with Jesus*, and the coauthor of *Lent: One Day at a Time for Catholic Teens*, *Advent and Christmas: One Day at a Time for Catholic Teens*, and *First Reconciliation and Beyond: A Family's Guide for Learning and Living Forgiveness*.

Prejean McGrady also serves as host of the *Like a Mother* podcast and cohost of *Family Mass Prep* on the Hallow app. She writes for several outlets, including Blessed is She, *Our Sunday Visitor*, and *Aleteia*, and contributes coverage on the Vatican and Church news to CNN. Prejean McGrady has spoken at the National Catholic Youth Conference, Steubenville Youth Conferences, and the Los Angeles Religious Education Congress, as well as in dioceses and parishes throughout the world.

Prejean McGrady earned a theology degree from the University of Dallas.

She lives in Lake Charles, Louisiana, with her husband Tommy and their children.

katieprejeanmcgrady.com
Facebook: @katiepmcgrady
Instagram: @katiepmcgrady
X: @KatiePMcGrady

Tommy McGrady is a biology teacher at Lake Charles College Prep in Louisiana, cohost of *Family Mass Prep* on the Hallow app, and a parish coach for the Accompaniment Project with the National Federation for Catholic Youth Ministry. He is the author of Life Teen's *Unleashed: Men of Scripture* and coauthor of *Lent: One Day at a Time for Catholic Teens*, *Advent and Christmas: One Day at a Time for Catholic Teens*, and *First Reconciliation and Beyond: A Family's Guide for Learning and Living Forgiveness*.

He has spoken at a number of youth rallies, youth ministry trainings, and diocesan events throughout the country.

In 2016, McGrady earned a distinguished young alumni award from Eastern University, where he obtained a bachelor's degree in biology in 2010. In 2023, he completed his master's degree in educational administration. McGrady previously served as the coordinator of youth and young adult ministry in the Diocese of Scranton and as a campus minister and theology teacher at St. Louis Catholic High School in Lake Charles, Louisiana.

He lives in Lake Charles, Louisiana, with his wife Katie Prejean McGrady and their children.

Facebook: @tommy.mcgrady
Instagram: @tmcgrady25
X: @tmcgrady25

Go Beyond the Book!

This special video series from the McGrady family brings key themes from the book to life with **practical insights**, **real-life stories**, and **spiritual encouragement for families**.

Designed specifically for parents, educators, and kids—with a special bonus episode for priests!

FOLLOW ON
Hallow

You can also find the McGradys' exclusive series on Hallow, the #1 Catholic prayer and mediation app, where they offer faith-filled reflections to help families grow closer to God—and to each other.

Scan here to watch or visit **hallow.com/collections/2696**.